Galatians

INTERPRETATION
A Bible Commentary for Teaching and Preaching

INTERPRETATION
A BIBLE COMMENTARY FOR TEACHING AND PREACHING

James Luther Mays, *Editor*
Patrick D. Miller, Jr., *Old Testament Editor*
Paul J. Achtemeier, *New Testament Editor*

CHARLES B. COUSAR

Galatians

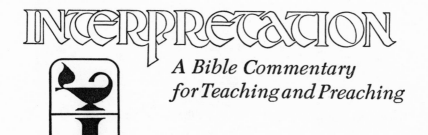

A Bible Commentary
for Teaching and Preaching

John Knox Press
ATLANTA

Scripture quotations are from the Revised Standard Version of the
Holy Bible, copyright, 1946, 1952, and © 1971, 1973 by the Division
of Christian Education, National Council of the Churches of Christ in
the U.S.A. and used by permission.

Library of Congress Cataloging in Publication Data

Cousar, Charles B.
  Galatians: a Bible commentary for teaching
and preaching.

  (Interpretation, a Bible commentary for teaching
and preaching.
  Bibliography: p.
  1. Bible. N.T. Galatians—Commentaries.
I. Title. II. Series.
BS2685.C64   227'.407   81–82354
ISBN 0–8042–3138–9   AACR2

© copyright John Knox Press 1982
10 9 8 7 6 5 4 3 2 1
Printed in the United States of America
John Knox Press
Atlanta, Georgia 30365

SERIES PREFACE

This series of commentaries offers an interpretation of the books of the Bible. It is designed to meet the need of students, teachers, ministers, and priests for a contemporary expository commentary. These volumes will not replace the historical critical commentary or homiletical aids to preaching. The purpose of this series is rather to provide a third kind of resource, a commentary which presents the integrated result of historical and theological work with the biblical text.

An interpretation in the full sense of the term involves a text, an interpreter, and someone for whom the interpretation is made. Here, the text is what stands written in the Bible in its full identity as literature from the time of "the prophets and apostles," the literature which is read to inform, inspire, and guide the life of faith. The interpreters are scholars who seek to create an interpretation which is both faithful to the text and useful to the church. The series is written for those who teach, preach, and study the Bible in the community of faith.

The comment generally takes the form of expository essays. It is planned and written in the light of the needs and questions which arise in the use of the Bible as Holy Scripture. The insights and results of contemporary scholarly research are used for the sake of the exposition. The commentators write as exegetes and theologians. The task which they undertake is both to deal with what the texts say and to discern their meaning for faith and life. The exposition is the unified work of one interpreter.

The text on which the comment is based is the Revised Standard Version of the Bible. The general availability of this translation makes the printing of a translation unnecessary and saves the space for comment. The text is divided into sections appropriate to the particular book; comment deals with passages as a whole, rather than proceeding word by word, or verse by verse.

Writers have planned their volumes in light of the requirements set by the exposition of the book assigned to them. Biblical books differ in character, content, and arrangement. They also differ in the way they have been and are used in the liturgy, thought, and devotion of the church. The distinctiveness and use of particular books have been taken into account in decisions about the approach, emphasis, and use of space in the commentaries. The goal has been to allow writers to develop the format which provides for the best presentation of their interpretation.

The result, writers and editors hope, is a commentary which both explains and applies, an interpretation which deals with both the meaning and the significance of biblical texts. Each commentary reflects, of course, the writer's own approach and perception of the church and world. It could and should not be otherwise. Every interpretation of any kind is individual in that sense; it is one reading of the text. But all who work at the interpretation of Scripture in the church need the help and stimulation of a colleague's reading and understanding of the text. If these volumes serve and encourage interpretation in that way, their preparation and publication will realize their purpose.

The Editors

PREFACE

The plan for this commentary is simple. Like Gaul, the letter is divided into three major divisions, which in turn provide the rationale and structure for the three parts of the commentary. At the beginning of each part, attention is given to the outline of the entire section, and then passage-by-passage comments on the text follow. No attempt has been made to solve all of the problems which arise in the course of a careful investigation of the letter. The primary task is to clarify the logic of Paul's line of argument and to reflect on the theology emerging from the text. Three passages warrant special consideration: 1:15–16; 2:15–21; 3:26–29. Each is treated in a separate way. The Introduction deals with the historical situation surrounding the writing of Galatians, sketches briefly the structure of the letter, and offers a summary statement of its theological import.

The commentary is based on the Revised Standard Version (RSV). I have regularly consulted four other English translations and from time to time cite them for clarity or contrast. They are The New English Bible (NEB), the Jerusalem Bible (JB), Today's English Version (TEV, sometimes referred to as the Good News Bible), and the New International Version (NIV).

Since references to other works on Galatians have been kept to a minimum, the Bibliography at the conclusion is all the more important. It is composed of one section recommending items for further study (annotated) and another listing the full bibliographical information on other sources cited in the commentary. Unfortunately the major study of Galatians by Hans Dieter Betz in the HERMENEIA series appeared too late to be given serious consideration in the commentary itself.

I am indebted to a number of people other than those mentioned in the Bibliography. The Board of Directors of Columbia Theological Seminary gave me a sabbatical leave from teaching duties, and a research grant from the Association of Theological Schools in the United States and Canada made possible an enjoyable year at Westminster College, Cambridge, England, where I did most of the writing. I particularly appreciate the support of J. Davison Philips. Students at Columbia with whom I have studied Galatians through the years have contributed more than they realize to this book through their own perceptive insights into the issues of the letter. The commentary would have been much the worse without the steady support and extremely helpful suggestions of the editors of the series. Two friends, A. M. Hunter and S. C. Guthrie, Jr., also kindly read portions of the manuscript and by their comments substantially strengthened the final product. My first teachers, Irving B. and R. Wilbur Cousar, initially sparked my interest in the New Testament by faithfully demonstrating in deed and in word what the text really means. Betty, my wife, who has not read a word of copy, has done more than anyone to see this project to completion. She has the inexplicable knack of knowing when to prod the procrastinator in me and when to encourage the frustrated. For all these people I am grateful.

Charles B. Cousar

CONTENTS

To
Betty

INTRODUCTION

Paul's letter to the Galatians has had an impact on the life and thought of the Christian church far exceeding its modest length. Though less than 150 verses (compared to more than 1000 in Acts, nearly 870 in the Gospel of John, and 303 in Hebrews), it has exercised a profound influence on theologians struggling with the issues of freedom and faith, gospel and law, the Spirit and ethics. In the second century when Marcion developed his controversial canon of NT books, he divided it into two sections: Gospel and Apostle. Galatians, for theological reasons, headed the list in the latter section. During the patristic period commentaries on Galatians seem to have been more numerous than on any other of Paul's letters. The influence of the epistle on Martin Luther is well known. He found it immediately relevant to the situation of the church in the sixteenth century and wrote unquestionably the most influential commentary on the letter. John Calvin took an interest in Galatians, too, but his commentary is less a theological treatise and more a practical exposition of the text. During the nineteenth century Galatians became the focal point of a discussion on the history of the early church, in which Paul as spokesman for Gentile Christianity was set in sharp conflict with the original apostles. Galatians 2, containing the report of the meeting between Paul and the Jerusalem leaders and the confrontation with Peter at Antioch, was subjected to close examination. More recently, interpreters have found in Galatians clarification about the meaning of justification by faith, help with the identity and character of the people of God, and guidance for the responsible use of freedom. The epistle contains the strongest statement of the equality of females and males to be found in the NT (3:28).

The intention of this commentary is to follow as closely as possible the message Paul wrote to the Galatians in the first century and, in doing so, to discern theological overtones appropriate for the church and the world of the present. The development of particular motifs in connection with passages is not meant to delimit or constrict the interpreter, but to be suggestive. Much more could and should be written about the implications of the text. But even to mention theology is to raise a special problem.

1

What specific theological overtones are picked up and how they are elaborated are partly determined by the "hearing" of the commentator. It is impossible to deny that the author of this commentary listens to the text as a particular person upon whose thinking all the influences of his identity and experience play. That is nothing new. The Bible is always interpreted in one set of historical circumstances or another. The question is, What can the listener do to gain some leverage on himself or herself so that the theological overtones are not grossly distorted and the freedom of the word of God is fully acknowledged? Two things are necessary. First, it is important to determine as clearly as possible the meaning of the text to the original readers. The historical-critical method of exegesis is intended to assist in doing just that. While it certainly does not guarantee that a theologically fruitful interpretation will result, it must be consistently employed in the search for such an interpretation. Unfortunately a scarcity of information often results in tenuous conclusions. Instead of deciding, for instance, exactly who the persons were who perverted the gospel in their preaching (1:6–7), one may only be able to suggest alternate possibilities. Honesty and caution in historical research are the better parts of wisdom. Nevertheless, descriptive work helps in reading the text objectively and in guiding the twentieth century listener who seeks a word from the Lord. Secondly, it is important to be open to others who have read and interpreted Galatians. Especially those of different ethnic, sexual, and theological backgrounds can often provide a different slant on the meaning of the text. The giants of the past, while writing in and for dissimilar contexts, nevertheless represent insights which in many cases have stood the test of time. It is through the community of interpreters as well as through one's personal encounter with the epistle that one dares to anticipate the authentic voice of the Spirit.

Before turning to the commentary itself, we need by way of introduction to consider three critical issues. The first has to do with the historical circumstances surrounding the writing of the letter. Who wrote Galatians? To whom was it written? What was the author's relationship to the readers? What specific situation evoked the letter? And when was it written? Secondly, it is essential to examine the overall structure of the document to gain a sense of the movement of thought from beginning to end. Finally, there is the matter of the theological significance

2

of the letter. Will a careful study of Galatians lead only to an understanding of first century issues, or can the contemporary reader expect to find help with the needs of faith and life today?

Historical Circumstances

1. The epistle bears the name of Paul as author (1:1), and no piece of information from within the document itself or from the early tradition of the church seriously calls into question Pauline authorship. The statement in 6:11 ("See with what large letters I am writing to you with my own hand") suggests that the major portion of the document was actually written by an amanuensis, as was Paul's custom, and only the conclusion was originally in his own script (cf. 1 Cor. 16:21). The autobiographical comments in the first two chapters provide more information on Paul's whereabouts from the time of his call on the Damascus Road to the time of the letter than do any other of his writings.

2. A clear definition of where the recipients of the letter lived is less possible than the decision about authorship. The Galatians originally were Celts who had immigrated into central Asia Minor in approximately 285 B.C. and had as their primary cities Ancyra, Pessinus, and Tavium. Later at the time of the Roman conquests, the territory of Galatia was annexed to the empire and in 25 B.C. was expanded to become a Roman province. Included in the expansion were several districts in southern Asia Minor—Pisidia and parts of Lycaonia and Phrygia. When Paul addresses his letter "to the churches of Galatia" (1:2), does he mean the churches of the original Galatian territory or to the churches of the expanded Roman province? The letter itself gives little help of a specific nature in solving the problem, except the information that Paul had visited the churches at least once, and perhaps twice, prior to writing (1:8; 4:13–15). If by "Galatia" he meant the Roman province, then Paul founded churches in the area (i.e., in Pisidian Antioch, Iconium, Lystra, and Derbe) on his first missionary journey (Acts 13—14) and visited them again on his second missionary journey (Acts 16:1–5). If by "Galatia" he meant the original territory of central Asia Minor, then Paul passed through the region on his second missionary journey (Acts 16:6) and on his third journey nurtured congregations which were already there (Acts 18:23).

It is frankly very difficult to determine with certainty for

3

which of these two areas the letter was originally intended. The theory which takes Galatia to be the more limited territory of central Asia Minor presents fewer problems of interpretation. It seems more in line with the way other geographical terms are used in the epistle, such as Syria, Judea, and Arabia. While it is true that the chief cities in the territory are not mentioned in Acts, this should not be taken too seriously, since Acts clearly does not provide a complete account of Paul's travels. Fortunately, however, the decision as to exactly where the recipients lived does not substantially affect the interpretation of the contents. It is only on the even more uncertain question of the dating of the letter that the determination of "Galatia" has any bearing.

3. At this point, however, it is important to reconstruct Paul's relationship with the churches of Galatia prior to the writing of the epistle. His initial stay in the area was in part connected with a physical ailment, the details of which are rather obscure. The Galatians received him warmly and were in no way put off by his difficulties. They accepted him "as an angel of God, as Christ Jesus" and were prepared to make great sacrifices to tend to his needs (4:13–15). He preached the gospel to them; they responded with much enthusiasm. Crucial to their experience of those early days in the faith was the active presence of the Spirit in the believing community, accompanied by the working of miracles. Paul could later appeal to the memory of their Christian beginnings in order to encourage their faithfulness to the call of grace (3:1–5; 1:6–9). Sometime after his first or perhaps second visit to Galatia other itinerant missionaries arrived and began to advocate a different message. In addition to preaching Christ, they urged that the predominantly Gentile congregations adopt the Jewish practice of circumcision in order to secure themselves a place among the people of God. Thereby the Christian experience could be brought to perfection. The Galatians, struggling with the demands of living out their calling in a pagan environment, were no doubt vulnerable to the security and guarantees offered in the message of circumcision. Many likely responded in a positive manner.

4

Paul, hearing of the situation, addresses this epistle to the congregations of Galatia. He expresses his astonishment that they could be persuaded by the teaching of the agitators and makes his case for the gospel of grace. To submit to circumcision is to turn one's back on the freedom given in Christ in favor of a rite which no longer has relevance and can only lead back to slavery (1:6–9; 3:1; 4:8–11; 5:6; 6:15). Whether the Galatian Christians heeded Paul's words or not is a matter of conjecture.

4. Who were the itinerant missionaries who in Paul's absence had such an influence on the Galatians? Paul refers to them as agitators, trouble-makers, who had a selfish motive in advocating circumcision. From his vantage point they were more interested in making a good showing for themselves and in avoiding persecution than they were in the welfare of the Galatian Christians (1:7; 4:17; 5:10; 6:12–13).

A number of attempts have been made through the years ro identify the agitators, and it is worth listing the more important suggestions.

(a) They were Jewish Christians from Jerusalem, representatives of a circumcision party within that church and claiming the support of James. They argued that the ceremonial laws were still in force and attacked Paul's renegade tendencies in preaching a radical message of freedom.

(b) They were Jewish Christians, but with no specific support from the Jewish authorities in Jerusalem. Paul's preaching was adequate as far as it went, but needed supplementing by the requirement of circumcision. By gaining converts from otherwise uncircumcised Christians, they avoided harrassment from zealous fellow-Jews.

(c) They were Jewish Christians of gnostic persuasion, who did not care about the law as such and operated in total independence of the Jerusalem church. The advocacy of circumcision and calendar observances (4:10) developed out of the syncretistic character of their religion.

(d) They were not Jews at all, but Gentile Christians. They felt that Paul's preaching, in line with the practice of the church at Jerusalem, had initially included circumcision. But under pressure Paul had changed his message. Thus they had to take up the cause of Judaism out of loyalty to the Jerusalem leaders.

(e) The opposition was composed of two groups. One group included judaizing activists who urged submission to the law; the other was made up of radicals of the opposite stripe, spiritualists who felt themselves exempt from moral issues. Paul addressed the former group in the first four-and-a-half chapters of the letter and the latter group in the final chapter-and-a-half.

An adequate evaluation of these identifications would lead

5

far beyond the scope of this Introduction. Each theory concentrates on one or more clues from the letter, but each also has difficulty in explaining all the data. The second (b), however, presents the most plausible description of who the opponents were and why they were active in the Galatian congregations. It does not perceive in the controversy a power struggle between the Jerusalem church and Paul, but it recognizes that one of the issues at stake does substantially relate to the place of the Gentiles in a church that has Jewish roots. At various places in the commentary it will be necessary to reflect further on the identity and activity of the agitators. (See on 1:6–10, the opening section to Part III, and 6:12–13.)

5. When was the letter to the Galatians written? The response depends on the solution to several previous questions, none of which can be answered unambiguously.

(a) Had Paul paid one or two visits to Galatia prior to writing the letter? Verse 13 of chapter 4 can be interpreted to imply two visits, though such an interpretation is not mandatory.

(b) Does the visit to Jerusalem (reported in 2:1–10) parallel the meeting of leaders mentioned in Acts 15? If so, then the letter obviously must have been written after that meeting, though how far after is uncertain. If the visit to Jerusalem in 2:1 predates the one mentioned in Acts 15, then the letter must have an early dating—toward the end of the first missionary journey.

(c) Did Paul write to provincial Galatia or to territorial Galatia? If he wrote to provincial Galatia, then according to Acts he visited the towns there on his first journey (perhaps even twice, Acts 13—14) and had another visit on his second journey (Acts 16:1–5). The letter could have been written any time after the concluding portion of the first journey. If he wrote to territorial Galatia, the first visit would have come on his second missionary journey (Acts 16:6) and his second visit on the third journey (Acts 18:23). The letter, then, could not have been written before the stop at Ephesus on the third journey.

In light of these uncertainties, fixing a specific time is hazardous. A few commentators date the letter as early as A.D. 49 on the basis that the letter was written to provincial Galatia and the visit to Jerusalem (2:1–10) comes before the meeting in Acts 15. The latest possible date would be A.D. 56, toward the end of the third missionary journey. A judicious guess would say that the letter originated sometime between A.D. 53 and 55, prior to or contemporary with the Corinthian letters but before the writing of Romans. It is obviously impossible to locate Paul at the time of writing. Suggestions have included Ephesus, Corinth, Macedonia, and in the case of the very early dating, Antioch.

Structure

Galatians is written with emotion and intensity. Paul does not hide his feelings of frustration and anguish for his readers (1:6; 3:1; 4:16, 19–20; 5:7) nor his anger toward the agitators (5:10–12). Still, the letter is orderly. Its argument flows in a rational pattern from beginning to end. A recent commentator has even suggested that Galatians is a clear example of the literary *genre* called the "apologetic letter" and that the various components carefully follow the patterns of classical rhetoric (H.D. Betz, *Galatians,* HERMENEIA, pp. 14–33). Be that as it may, the document was not haphazardly thrown together.

Details of the structure are discussed in the opening sections to each of the three parts of the commentary. Here it is important to get a sense of the larger picture. Following the introduction to the letter in which the author identifies himself and greets his readers, the body is divided into three major segments. In the first (1:6—2:21) Paul clarifies his reason for writing and in doing so begins to build his case for dealing with the problems in the congregations. The fundamental task is to remind the Galatians of the supreme authority of the gospel of grace—an authority which led them to faith (1:6,9), which redirected Paul's life and set him to evangelize the Gentiles (1:11–17), which formed the basis of the unity acknowledged at Jerusalem (2:1–10), and which in one specific episode judged Peter (2:14). The priority of grace means that God's justification is not determined by the law, that is, it is not restricted to Jews and other law-abiding people. It is received by faith (2:15–21).

In the second major division (3:1—5:12), Paul continues his case by reminding the Galatians of their own origin as Christians (3:1–5), a beginning which had been marked by the preaching of Christ and the response of faith. But this stress on the unmerited grace of the gospel leads Paul to face two crucial questions: Who constitutes the people of God (i.e., who are the true children of Abraham), and what is the function of the law (3:6—5:1)? Paul deals with these questions by frequent reference to Old Testament texts which he views as pointing to the

7

Christ-event and to the inclusion of non-Jews. To be a child of
freedom is not to trace one's genetic line back to Abraham,
which the offspring of Hagar could do, but to be a child of
promise, born according to the Spirit (4:22–31). The section is
completed with a personal appeal to the readers (5:2–12).

The third major division (5:13—6:10) addresses the responsible use of freedom. Enthusiastic experiences of the Spirit
often lead to excess and to overlooking the moral leadership of
the Spirit. This may have been the situation in Galatia since in
the midst of his comments on the Spirit Paul specifically mentions bickering and jealousy (5:15, 26). Instead of offering a set
of rules and regulations, he reminds the readers of the primary
fruit of the Spirit—love, which fulfills the law and builds community (5:13–14,22). Love leads beyond legalism to a concern
for the fallen brother or sister who needs help in the bearing of
burdens (6:1–2). Thus those who through the Spirit have been
given life are exhorted to conduct their lives in accordance with
the same Spirit (5:25). The letter concludes with a personal
postscript in which the cross of Christ is made the yardstick for
life, exposing any effort, religious or otherwise, to supplement
the grace of God (6:11–18). This represents a motif which plays
a prominent role throughout the letter (2:19–20; 5:11, 24).

Theological Significance

At the beginning of the Introduction the point was made
that Galatians has had an influence on the life and thought of
the church far exceeding its modest length. Both heretics and
orthodox theologians have been profoundly shaped by Paul's
succinct message written in a highly polemical context. What
has been the appeal of Galatians? What is the theological thrust
of the letter? Does it have continuing meaning for Christian
people whose lives are far removed from Galatia and the pressure to conform to a religious practice like circumcision? The
commentary seeks to answer such questions, but it is essential
to offer here a preliminary statement.

The theological excitement of Galatians lies in the radical
interpretation Paul makes of the meaning of God's grace. It is
more than a doctrine; it is an experience. At the same time, it
8   is *the* doctrine which undergirds all that Paul fights for in this
letter. The agitators who come into the Galatian congregations
are not opposed to the idea that God is gracious. It is just that
grace is only part of the story. Faith, the human response

to grace, begins a process which circumcision completes.

Before examining Paul's attack on the theology of the agitators, we need to see the attraction their position held for the Galatians. There were probably three appealing features. First, circumcision provided a measure of security, a visible sign that the one circumcised truly was a member of God's family. For a male Gentile who entered a religious community which traced its origins back to Abraham, this was not an inconsequential matter. Circumcision identified him as one of the people of God and represented a far more tangible sign than mere faith could ever do. Secondly, circumcision as presented to the Galatians was a symbolic act intended to lead to full maturity. The removal of a piece of flesh by a surgical procedure signified a mastery over the power of the flesh and thus a moving on toward perfection. In a pagan environment where coping with moral problems was extremely difficult for Christian converts, such a religious rite offered help. (See the commentary on 3:3.) Finally, circumcision seemed to be a step to take in order to fulfill the Old Testament commandments. It was a clearly defined requirement of the divine law (Gen. 17:9–14). Surely God would honor obedience to his will.

Paul does not confront the teaching of the agitators in a pragmatic fashion, carefully determining what type of argument might succeed in bringing them around to his position. An accommodating stance, a "Yes, but . . ." answer is missing from Galatians. The reason is not that Paul is stubborn and dogmatic, but that he perceives how completely his readers have misunderstood the heart of the Christian faith. They are working at the wrong end of the relationship with God—what *they* can do to assure inclusion in God's family; what *they* can do to cope with the power of the flesh; what *they* can do to fulfill the law. The answer lies at the other end—what *God* has done in Christ and how he has done it. "Grace," a word occurring at six key points in the letter, is not a "thing," even a "thing" God gives. Rather it describes the manner in which God gives himself, the personal relationship he establishes with his people. The word depicts the unmerited and unconditional way in which God has made and continues to make his move toward sinful humanity. "God sent forth his Son, . . . to redeem those who were under the law, so that we might receive adoption as sons" (4:4–5). Given that reality, there can be no compromise with any other means of dealing with the law or gaining membership in God's

9

family, no middle ground where God does his part and humans do their part.

Paul's vigorous statement of God's radical grace may be hard to grasp in the twentieth century because of the familiarity of the language. The terms have not only become a part of the church's liturgy; they have also been thoroughly adopted by the prevailing culture. (Notice how frequently the verb "believe" occurs in modern advertising and that a recording of "Amazing Grace" made the Top Twenty.) Yet the doctrine of grace continues to exercise a polemical function, especially in an achievement-oriented society where handouts are either suspect or expected. Circumcision has its religious and secular counterparts in the various ways in which we "supplement" God's free gift of himself and prescribe for ourselves (or others) a particular accomplishment which becomes a "must." A piety which turns into anxiety about one's own (or another's) spiritual health and searches for unforgiven sins has forgotten what God has done in Christ and how he has done it. It is an example of starting at the wrong end of the relationship.

There are three prominent points at which Paul's understanding of grace comes to expression in Galatians.

1. The issue of circumcision can be put another way. Do Gentiles have to become Jews in order to be full-fledged Christians? Paul's answer is an unequivocal "No." The very nature of grace eliminates special categories. It provides for a commonality based on something other than ethnic, social, or sexual distinctions. "There is neither Jew nor Greek, there is neither slave nor free, there is neither male nor female; for you are all one in Christ Jesus" (3:28). The superior-inferior relationship otherwise observed in each of these pairs disappears in the light of God's unconditional mercy in Christ. A new unity based on the gospel emerges. (See the commentary on 2:1–10 and 3:26–29.)

2. What is the appropriate human response to grace? It is, of course, faith—the sometimes quiet, sometimes reckless confidence in the goodness and faithfulness of God. Such confidence is rooted in the death and resurrection of Christ as the supreme expression of God's grace. This means that faith is not a way for humans to "get God on their side." He is already *for* them. In faith they change, not he. The experience of trusting God always leads to the thorough reshaping of the believer—what Paul described as "a new creation" (6:15). Leander E. Keck comments:

10

When Paul called for trust, then, he was calling for reconfiguration of the self. To trust God as presented in the message of the cross/resurrection and of Jesus' Lordship and coming, is to challenge the previous configurations of trust and their ground. If one rejects the gospel, one maintains the status quo; if one accepts the message, one begins to realign that configuration—one heeds the message, 'obeys' the gospel . . . The only way one can heed the news of God's grace is to entrust oneself to this God. (*Paul and His Letters,* p. 53).

3. A grace which evokes faith leads to love. This is the progression within Galatians. First Paul establishes the authority of the gospel of grace; then he sets faith over against "works of the law"; and finally he affirms that the proper exercise of the life of faith (freedom) is loving service to one's neighbor. This stress on God's spontaneous and lavish self-giving is not to be confused with permissiveness or maudlin sentimentality. The God who gives himself is the God who is not to be mocked (6:7), and the love which fulfills the law is the love active amidst dissension, pride, and envy (5:14–15, 26). It takes shape in the restoration of the fallen and never wearies of doing good to all (6:1,9–10).

PART ONE

Grace and the Liberating Authority of the Gospel

GALATIANS 1:1 — 2:21

The structure of the first major section of Galatians is straightforward. Paul begins (1:1–5) in the pattern typical of the epistolary form, in which he identifies authors and readers and offers a word of salutation. It becomes immediately obvious that though the form is a recognizably established one he uses it to address the issue in the communities in Galatia and to lay the theological foundation for what is to follow. Compared with other Pauline introductions, this one reveals a distressing situation in which relations between author and reader are strained.

Instead of offering the usual prayer of thanksgiving for his readers (1:6–10), Paul expresses his amazement at the sudden defection of the Galatian Christians to a position contrary to the gospel they had previously accepted. They were encouraged by the agitators to think that the practice of circumcision was a needful complement to belief in Christ. But with two anathemas Paul insists on the binding authority of the one gospel, already preached and received. Verse 10 provides a transition to the next section (acknowledged in the RSV with 1:10 as a separate paragraph) by setting up the alternative of "pleasing men" or "being a servant of Christ," an alternative paralleled in 1:11–12 by the reception of the gospel from a human source or "by a revelation of Jesus Christ."

Beginning at verse 11 and continuing through verse 21, of chapter 2, Paul relates a significant piece of his own history in order to lay emphasis on the divine origin of the gospel. First,

13

he describes his days of religious zeal in Judaism, which were interrupted by the call of God to preach Christ to the Gentiles (1:13–16a). What he did immediately following the call was to go to Arabia and then to Damascus (1:16b–17). Only after three years did he go to Jerusalem for a two-week visit with Peter (1:18–20). There was no public meeting nor major consultation on that trip. The point Paul wants to make is that he preached the gospel in such a way that good things happened (1:22–24), but he was not doing so as a disciple or emissary of the Jerusalem authorities. His commission comes from God and not from Jerusalem.

Paul tells about a second visit to Jerusalem (2:1–10), more official and formal, when he carried with him two of his missionary companions, Barnabas and Titus. The account of the meeting is important to Paul's argument in Galatians because he can report an agreement about the character of the gospel and thus about the basis for the unity of the church. James, Peter, and John recognized the message of freedom he was preaching and the direction of his mission among the Gentiles.

This acknowledgement, however, did not mean that all the problems of the church were instantly solved. Thus Paul records still another personal experience (2:11–14), this time one of conflict. Peter who at Antioch had for a time eaten with Gentiles ceased doing so when faced with a group from Jerusalem. Paul confronted him directly over his action and vigorously contended for the rights of non-Jews in the church (2:14). The issue for Paul is a theological one, and the incident provides the context to state his understanding of justification by grace and of being crucified with Christ. If justification had come in any other way, Christ's death would have been needless (2:15–21). These concluding reflections then are picked up and elaborated in the second major part of the epistle beginning with chapter three.

Crucial to an understanding of this initial section is the observation that the noun "gospel" and the verb "preach" (i.e., the particular Greek word which has "gospel" as its root) occur thirteen times in these two chapters (plus several other occasions where pronouns are used for which "gospel" is the antecedent). But more important than the word-count are the decisive contexts in which the words appear (1:6–9, 11–12, 16,23; 2:2, 7,14). The fundamental problem with the Galatians is not their rejection of Paul or his apostleship, but their alteration of

14

the gospel. The message originally preached to them, which they had received, is the gospel Paul himself received "through a revelation of Jesus Christ" (1:12). It is the reason why he resisted the pressure to have Titus circumcised (2:3) and what in fact the Jerusalem apostles acknowledged (2:7). When Peter was challenged at Antioch, it was because he was not "straight-forward about the truth of the gospel" (2:14). If in the pages of the commentary the word "gospel" appears with great regular-ity, it is because of the dominant role it plays in these first two chapters.

Galatians 1:1–5
An Important Beginning

A study of the beginning of Paul's letters is a profitable enterprise. One might mistakenly assume that because the apostle at the outset closely follows the style of letter-writing of his day and uses stereotyped phrases and prescriptive for-mulas the first verses can be advantageously skipped or, at least, run through quickly. As a matter of fact, however, his letters do not all begin the same way. The descriptive phrases Paul uses to introduce himself, the initial tone with which he addresses his readers, and the contents of the greeting vary a great deal from letter to letter. Paul follows a stylized form, but with such variety that the reader can often get a clue as to what is coming in the body of the letter and can find in the introduction phrases and clauses rich with theological import.

The structure of the introduction to the Galatian letter is no different from the structure of the other Pauline letters: from Paul (sender); to the churches of Galatia (readers); grace to you and peace (greeting). And yet the manner in which these three components are elaborated (or not elaborated, as in the case of the readers) makes the Galatian introduction like no other. For example, Paul's apostleship is affirmed first by a denial. Not from a human source or through a human mediator does he claim the apostolic authority to write as he does to the Galatians, but through Jesus Christ himself and God, "who raised him from the dead" (1:1). Immediately an

15

issue surfaces. The opponents in Galatia have either deliberately set out to undermine the authenticity of Paul's message
by declaring his apostleship an inferior one, or, more likely,
they have implied as much by the manner and content of
their own preaching. Paul departs from the self-designations
most familiar to us from his other epistles, for example, "a servant of Jesus Christ, called to be an apostle" (Rom. 1:1; cf.
Phil. 1:1), "an apostle of Jesus Christ" by the will of God (II
Cor. 1:1; cf. I Cor. 1:1). Instead he sets about right away to
engage his opponents by clarifying the source of his authority,
a concern which occupies much of the first two chapters. One
cannot, then, hastily bypass the introduction without missing
an integral piece of the argument.

But the introduction bears careful scrutiny for a more important reason. The elaborated greeting provides the theological starting point for Paul's thinking in this letter and summa-
rizes the message which occupies the end of the second and
most of the final four chapters. Jesus Christ is identified as the
one "who gave himself for our sins to deliver us from the
present evil age, according to the will of our God and Father"
(1:4). The reason Paul so vehemently attacks the agitators who
operate in the Galatian communities with their message of circumcision lies in his conviction that there is no salvation except
in the crucified Christ. The legalist, whether of the first century
or the twentieth, errs precisely in presupposing, consciously or
not, that the death of Christ is insufficient and must be aug-
mented. Paul contends that "if righteousness comes by law,
then Christ died for nothing" (2:21, NEB). The apostle starts,
then, not with an analysis of the world with its dire needs nor
with individuals and their self-consciousness but with Christ
and his saving act.

Look at the various components of this identification of
Christ. First, he *"gave himself for our sins"* (v.4). Normally Paul
uses the singular "sin" and so may in this verse (as in I Cor. 15:3)
be following a traditional formula; but in any case he clearly
relates the self-giving of Christ to our dark past, both as a community and as individuals. Christ's death has an expiatory
character, and that means, to change the metaphor, freedom
from the dismal shadow which yesterday so often casts over
today.

Frankly, talk of "sins" today often seems archaic. The word
in certain contexts takes on the character of jargon as the user

16

carefully avoids the difficulties of serious moral discussion about concrete issues. In like manner, the language of expiation seems quaint and unrelated. Perhaps the problem lies, in part, in the failure to grasp the extraordinary radicality in the phrase, "Christ died for our sins." This implies, among other things, that as our representative he has actually taken our place and assumed the responsibility for our irresponsibility, our complicity in the oppression of the weak, all our personal failures. We need no longer languish in our guilt nor pummel ourselves or one another with recriminations or remorse. Karl Barth has put it this way:

> But the great and inconceivable thing is that He acts as Judge in our place by taking upon Himself, by accepting responsibility for that which we do in this place. . . . And as he does that, it ceases to be our sin. It is no longer our affair to prosecute and represent this case. The right and possibility of doing so has been denied and taken away from us. What He in divine omnipotence did amongst us as one of us prevents us from being our own judges, from even wanting to be, from making that senseless attempt on the divine perogative, from sinning in that way and making ourselves guilty. In that He was and is for us that end is closed, and so is the evil way to that end. He is the man who entered that evil way, with the result that we are forced from it; it can be ours no longer (*Church Dogmatics,* Vol. IV, Part 1, p. 236).

Christ died for our sins, and thus we need no longer cling to them. Whatever guilt has done for us—protect us or haunt us —in the face of the gospel it is no more than a fleeting fantasy. "It is no longer our affair to prosecute and represent this case." Jacques Ellul comments, "Thus the past lives, not in the hell of my unconscious, but in the holiness of God" (*The Ethics of Freedom,* p. 140).

But the basic human question is not only what to do with our past sins, but how to cope with the conflicts of the present and the future. How can one be changed so that yesterday's errors are not repeated? Can the cycle of irresponsibility, complicity, and failure be broken? The salutation goes on to say that Christ died *"to deliver us from the present evil age."* Paul employs the eschatological language of Judaism to describe the current situation under the domination of evil in contrast to the (implied) age to come, characterized by freedom and hope (cf. I Cor. 2:6, 8; 3:18; Rom. 12:2; Eph. 1:21; 2:7). The stress here lies not on the chronology of the ages—when one begins and the other ends—since both exist simultaneously, but on the control-

17

ling power of the one from which rescue is needed. Whereas the language of "sins" suggests an expiatory view of the atonement, deliverance "from the present evil age" reflects the movement from one control to another based on participation with Christ in his death. It is the most prominent imagery in Galatians for the salvation-event (2:19–20; 3:23–26; 4:1–7, 8–9; 5:1; 6:14; cf. Rom. 6:5–11; 7:1–6; Eph. 2:1–10, etc.).

Though from an ancient thought-structure, Paul's language here has a more familiar ring. The feeling of being trapped, of being the pawn in the hands of a despotic chess player, of being caught by a power, whether experienced as an internal compulsion or an external force, is not strange. Such an enslavement prohibits a facing, much less a coping with, the moral dilemmas of present and future. It assures the repetition of yesterday's cycle. Its deterministic patterns can be broken only when a more potent authority steps in to deliver those who are hopelessly caught on a vicious treadmill. The death of Christ, Paul says, performs just this rescue operation and sets the liberated in the service of a new Lord (1:3). Not only is the past dealt with, but Christians are now under a control which empowers them for the present and future.

The elaborated greeting includes a third component. Christ "gave himself for our sins to deliver us from the present evil age, *according to the will of our God and Father.*" The phrase "the will of God" appears in the salutation of a number of epistles (I Cor. 1:1; II Cor 1:1; Eph. 1:1; Col. 1:1; II Tim. 1:1), and yet in all other instances it relates to the writer's status as apostle, whereas in Galatians it defines the saving work of Christ. In light of the controversy Paul addresses, it is important that he make clear that Christ's death was neither an accident nor a tragedy in the line of the martyr's sacrifice; it had to do with a larger, divine plan. The gospel had been announced beforehand to Abraham (3:8); only "when the time had fully come" did God send forth his son (4:4). Paul's own relationship with God began long before his birth (1:15). God had a purpose in the events of Good Friday to bring about the planned deliverance. To suggest, then, as the agitators at Galatia were doing, that Christ's death was insufficient and needed to be supplemented with further rites and rules was to advocate a position contrary to the will of God.

The foundation on which Paul builds his case is laid in the introduction to the letter. Theologically, the fault with the Gala-

18

tian heresy and any other expression of legalism is what it assumes, whether stated or not (and of course usually not), about
the meaning of the death of Christ. Is he adequate to cure the
paralysis resulting from human sins or is he not? Does he liberate from the domination of evil, or does he not? Is the death of
this one man really the means for dealing with the network of
broken relationships and the recurring cycle of destructive behavior which for so long have been a part of the human condition? This is the basic issue of the letter and one to which the
apostle will return in a variety of ways throughout the six chapters.

It is significant that nowhere in the beginning of this epistle
does Paul express his gratitude for or make a word of affirmation
about his readers. Galatians is the only Pauline letter in which
the traditional prayer of thanksgiving is omitted (cf. Rom.1:8–
15; I Cor. 1:4–9; Phil.1:3–11). At the point where such a prayer
would normally have come in the outline, Paul says, "I am
astonished that you are so quickly deserting him who called you
in the grace of Christ" (1:6). When believers are abandoning the
gospel for a perversion of the truth, the situation leaves him
little for which to be thankful. There is no reason to pretend
that things are better than they are. The issue is frankly grave.

Galatians 1:6–10
The Authority of the Gospel

As Paul moves from the introduction to the main body of
the letter and more directly addresses the situation in the Galatian congregations, the question of authority is immediately
raised. If there is conflict in the community, who will settle it,
and on what grounds? Is it to be a showdown between Paul's
status as a church leader and the status of his opponents? The
apparent success of the agitators, as Paul sees it, poses a threat
not to his personal position or reputation, but to the message of
grace. Thus in verses 6–10 he argues for the authority of the
gospel.

It may be well at the outset to note that from the time of
the New Testament onward the problem of authority has been
a serious one in the life of the church. On what basis are deci-

19

sions made and directions determined? Who calls the shots, and from where does one derive the right and power to call them? The presence of diverse theological positions and varying ecclesiastical traditions indicate that questions about authority linger. Perhaps the thorniest and at the same time most practical issue is not that of church polity—whether the church should be governed by bishops, a pope, elders, or the people— but the source to which the church goes to find solutions and settle disputes. Do the exigencies of the moment ("How are we going to pay for this?"), or internal needs ("But this will upset a lot of people!"), or age-old traditions ("We've always done it this way.") in the final analysis make the decisions and resolve the conflicts? The usual answer to the question of authority for those sensitive to theology of course is "church" or "Scripture." For Paul each has its appropriate place, but he points beyond each to a more antecedent authority (1:6–10).

Immediately following the salutation, the apostle expresses his consternation that some of the Galatian Christians (most of whom were Gentiles) have accepted the teaching of other preachers and have been persuaded that it is necessary to become a Jew in order to be a real Christian, that is, they have accepted the argument that circumcision is essential to salvation. Exactly who these preachers were is a matter of much dispute (See Introduction). Suffice it here to note that they were probably Christians of Jewish origin who lived in the Dispersion. There is no hint that they openly opposed the preaching of Christ; they thought that the preaching of Christ alone was insufficient.

But is this really a serious issue? Would it not be the better part of wisdom to thank God that they were not advocating sacred prostitution or divinely ordered sedition against Rome or something more destructive than circumcision? After all, circumcision was a rite established with Abraham; it had a good Old Testament precedent (cf. Gen. 17:9–14). For Paul, however, the issue is urgent. An addendum, when absolutized, negates the very nature of the gospel itself. What may seem like a harmless addition turns out to be a gross contradiction.

Antecedent even to the church and the Scripture, then, is the authority of the one gospel, which becomes the norm against which all theologies and other religious expressions are measured. Since the root word for "gospel" (noun and verb) occurs five times in 1:6–10, it is worth a closer look at the

20

affirmations made in this section as Paul works out his polemic against the agitators in Galatia. First, it is the gospel *of Christ* (1:7). The genitive in the Greek is probably intended to underscore the source and the content of the gospel. Neither democratic process nor due deliberation of church councils or courts decides whether the gospel has authority and what its content is to be. It comes from Christ and is about Christ (cf. Rom. 1:3). Just as he in his earthly ministry had exhibited a unique presence beyond which there was no appeal (cf. Mark 1:22; Matt. 7:29; Luke 4:32), so now his gospel exercises absolute authority in the church.

This raises a complicated issue. There are obviously those occasions when, as in the situation in Galatia, the gospel becomes domesticated. By the pervasive character of the culture, the political climate, the idiosyncracies of place or preacher, the gospel is taken over and transformed into an ideology. In the face of such occasions Paul's word here is apt. It is *Christ's* gospel, not capitalism's gospel, or the third world's gospel, or Rev. Smith's gospel. And yet, the gospel of which Paul speaks is not a series of fixed formulas to be translated precisely from the Greek into various languages and mechanically repeated time and again. Its implications and often its expression of necessity vary from culture to culture, political climate to political climate, place to place, and preacher to preacher. The good news needed to be heard by a capitalistic society may differ in its concreteness from the good news needed by the third world community. It will differ even from one capitalist to another. How then can one take account of such specific contexts and yet be sure that the gospel is not domesticated?

The fundamental nature of the gospel is grace. This was the issue in Galatia and remains so today—in simple terms, God's loving disposition and action in Christ toward his creation which had (and has) put itself in the grips of his enemy. The preaching of Christ's gospel will inevitably convey God's grace, not in an abstract or theoretical fashion, but in terms of the particular human situation. It may include judgment as well as mercy, imperative as well as indicative, and appropriately so, if arising from or leading to the word that God is *for* us. If there is a test to be applied to preaching, it is this: Does it declare Jesus Christ as the unqualified liberator—from religious legalism or secular cynicism, from paralyzing apathy or frantic anxiety, from being oppressed or being the oppressor, from cowardly

21

fear or brash self-reliance? And, as Paul will go on to say in Galatians, does this preaching clarify what Christ has freed us *for?*

Secondly, the gospel is more than a set of propositions about Christ, his death and resurrection (though obviously it can and must be so stated); *it is a divine activity by means of which people are drawn into the realm of God's grace.* Paul makes a surprising equation (1:6–7). The Galatians who depart from the message they had previously accepted and follow the theology of the agitators are deserting not merely a doctrine but God himself, "him who called you" (1:6). To abandon the gospel is to forsake God (cf. 5:4). Such an equation is possible because it was precisely in the preaching of the gospel that something had happened to and for the Galatians. They had been rescued out of "this present evil age" and set "in the grace of Christ" (1:6, taking the prepositional phrase as locative). The transfer from the control of one power to the dominion of another occurred in the preaching and receiving of the gospel. It then is a force effective in its own right which functions within history transforming persons, drawing them into the sway of grace. As authority, it functions not so much by setting boundaries and determining limits beyond which subjects cannot go (so most of the authorities familiar to us) as it does to effect change, to re-create, to fortify subjects for mission. P. T. Forsyth wrote about this authority:

> It is not, in the first instance, regulative and depressive; it is expansive, it is creative. Like personality, it is not a delimiting circle, but an exuberant source. It makes the soul to be more than in its egoism it could ever be. It means increase, augmentation. . . . Our great authority is what gives us most power to go forward; it is not what ties us up most to a formal past. It is of grace and not of law (*The Principle of Authority,* p. 13).

This means, then, that the authority of the gospel is different from the authority of a church's doctrinal statement or an officially approved position paper to which appeals concerning theology or ethics might be made. Such statements or position papers contain a legitimacy based on agreed-upon principles and processes, and interpretations in turn are made by appropriate persons. What authority the statements have derives from the body which approves them. The gospel, however, has a divine source; its authority is dynamic. In it an energy is released to change the plight of people and circumstances. Destructive patterns of life are broken and new ones established. "It is the power of God for salvation" (Rom. 1:16).

Now this may seem to put tremendous control in the hands of those who preach and in fact prove frightening—frightening to preachers who tremble at the thought of the responsibility and frightening to the laity who fear a clerical tyranny. For that reason, it is important to consider a third affirmation from the passage. *Those who preach (or teach) are singled out as being subject to the authority of the gospel.* Paul pronounces two curses. In the former he declares himself or any heavenly messenger accursed if either departs in his preaching from the gospel already preached. In the latter, he puts the agitators in Galatia under a curse if they abandon the gospel previously received by the Galatians. Verse 8 is not merely a rhetorical device but an important piece of Paul's argument in the pericope. It prevents the mistaken impression modern readers often get that Paul is personally under attack, becomes frantic and defensive about his own status, and selfishly fights for his apostolic prominence before the Galatians. Nowhere does Paul suggest that the community should be subordinated to him or that he needs to be revered in their eyes. It is not from him they are departing when they accept the agitators' teaching. He in fact is responsible to the same authority as that of the community—the gospel of Christ. If he changes his tone and departs from the gospel, he is no less cursed than the agitators themselves.

This should come as a welcome word for both preacher and congregation. The preacher, to be sure, assumes an awesome responsibility in daring to proclaim the gospel, but he or she need not suppose that the task week after week is to come up with a new gimmick to charm the congregation and somehow to be "more effective." If anything is to be genuinely effected, it will be through the preaching of the gospel. Of course that message has many ramifications; it speaks afresh in each new context. The preacher cannot repeat the same old sermon Sunday after Sunday and make excuse by citing 1:8. The task is to expose those numerous situations in human life and culture where God calls persons "from the present evil age" to the dominion of grace. Likewise the congregation need not fear a clerical tyranny. The absolute power of the gospel ultimately subdues any efforts to domesticate or control it. Like the wine Jesus spoke of, it will in time burst the old wineskins. It may

23

even transform that preacher who seeks to lord it over the congregation. In the final analysis, the preacher does not authenticate the gospel; the gospel authenticates the preacher.

The same holds true for the teacher as well. What gives any individual the right to teach within the context of the church is the gospel itself. It authorizes its own propagation and interpretation. Its liveliness gives credibility to the educational experience. To quote Forsyth again, the nature of such authority is not regulative or constricting. "Our great authority is what gives us most power to go forward. . . . It is of grace and not of law."

A brief comment on 1:10 can serve as a footnote to the above. Paul raises a question, seemingly with himself though aloud so that the Galatians can overhear. "Am I now seeking the favor of men, or of God?" It is a striking question to raise in a context where the issue is authority. Paul's answer is a reasoned deduction: "If I were still pleasing men, I should not be a servant of Christ." The human obligation to honor God and serve Christ is at the heart of the issue of authority and is reminiscent of Jesus' words in Matt. 20:25–28. All positions of leadership are in danger of becoming power bases where people satisfy their own needs, manipulate and even oppress others, and make certain that decisions turn out "our" way (never mind about God's way). In ecclesiastical circles the gospel may even be cleverly or unconsciously used to keep recalcitrants in line. Thus the simple question about service and accountability to God is always an appropriate question to ask oneself. Faced honestly, it will painfully expose human pretense, but at the same time will point toward true freedom.

Galatians 1:11–24
The Origin and Power of the Gospel in Paul's Life

With the exception of Paul's call, the section 1:11–24 usually arouses more interest from the historian seeking to develop a chronology of Paul's life than from the theologian seeking to preach. While a later section of the commentary deals with the call, three questions which arise about this section (1:11–24) need to be addressed in order to clarify the continuity of Paul's argument.

24

1. Why does the issue of apostleship figure so prominently in Paul's letter to the Galatians? Commentators do not agree on the answer to this question, and the disagreement stems, at least in part, from the fact that we hear only one side of the conversation Paul carries on with these congregations. Some (and perhaps the majority) contend that Paul is responding to charges made by his opponents in Galatia who say he is not a proper apostle. He has not been commisioned by the Jerusalem authorities and thus is a renegade advocating an unsanctioned message. Though he may have been originally instructed by the "pillar apostles," he has turned his back on them. Paul counters by affirming his independence as an apostle and by appropriately including in the narrative the Jerusalem meeting at which Peter, James, and John indicated their agreement with his teaching. The latter incident proves that his message of salvation to the Gentiles has their blessing. Other commentators agree that Paul is answering the personal attacks of his opponents, but say that he is being charged with total dependence on Jerusalem. What he expounds as the faith, he received at second or third hand. He was not an eyewitness of Jesus' ministry and could not be considered a real apostle. Paul's answer is to identify himself as an apostle who receives his commission from the *risen* Christ, to detail his whereabouts so as to prove independence from the Jerusalem apostles, and to report his public disagreement with Peter at Antioch.

The two groups of commentators agree in saying that the opponents raise the issue of apostleship. Paul is obliged to clear his name and status so that his message will not be discredited. They disagree, however, as to what the charges actually were. Was he a defector from or a pawn of Jerusalem? The difficulty lies in reconstructing an attack when the only available information comes from the refutation of this attack. A third group of commentators (and I am persuaded by their argument), however, raises a more basic question: Was there an attack at all? Is Paul defending himself from the insults of his opponents who question his apostleship, or does he raise the whole issue himself? The opponents advocate circumcision as essential to becoming a Christian, but do they, directly at least, assail his role as an apostle (as did the "false apostles" discussed in II Cor. 10—13)? Paul, it is suggested, is primarily interested in the one gospel, that it comes from God and thus functions as a divine power, and the issue of apostleship is introduced in order to clarify the question of apostolic *authority.* Paul does not fight

25

to open the circle of the Twelve and get himself admitted. He never provides a precise definition of an apostle, nor does he question the status of others so recognized. Even though he abruptly confronts Peter at Antioch, he does not initiate a campaign to oust Peter from his role as an apostle. The office *per se* is not the issue, nor is who is or who is not an apostle. The point Paul argues in Galatians is that any and all power apostles have derives from the one gospel; or to put it in the categories of J. H. Schutz' excellent study, Paul is not interested in legitimacy but in authority *(Paul and the Anatomy of Apostolic Authority)*. He reads like one on the offensive, not the defensive, as if he were attacking those who neglect his authority rather than responding to those who have made personal insults. The comment that he went to Jerusalem to present what he had been preaching among the Gentiles "lest somehow I should be running or had run in vain" (2:2) might suggest that Paul was uncertain about his message and was looking for confirmation or even correction from the Jerusalem apostles—an impossibility in light of the rest of the epistle. Rather than seeking to persuade them of his apostleship, Paul was more likely concerned about the unity of the church and whether the Jerusalem leaders were themselves subject to the gospel of grace. Evidently he was satisfied with the common source of their commission. "For God whose action made Peter an apostle to the Jews, also made me an apostle to the Gentiles" (2:8, NEB. The RSV obscures the issue with the translation "mission" rather than "apostle" or "apostleship."). In any case, whether Paul or his opponents raise the issue, apostleship is a concern bound up with the concern for the one gospel.

This issue, in one sense, is no longer relevant for the church. Apostles died out in the first century. In another sense (and really the Pauline sense), the issue continues. Paul speaks of the function of the apostle not in terms of guaranteeing the transmission and correct interpretation of the church's doctrine from one generation to another, but in terms of preaching the gospel. That function remains. What is affirmed about the priority of the gospel over the apostle can be affirmed in terms of the one who preaches or teaches. His or her authority (in distinction from legitimacy) is obtained neither from congregation nor ecclesiastical court but from the call of God through the gospel.

2. Why this extensive autobiographical material? Normally Paul is rather silent about himself and his travels; here he goes

into some detail and even with a vow attesting the sincerity of his report (1:20). First, he documents the statements made in verses 11–12 by indicating how he came to be a missionary among the Gentiles and where his early life as a Christian was spent. Paul knows he is not telling the Galatians something altogether new ("For you have heard of . . ." 1:13), but its rehearsal in this particular context is crucial. In no way has he been dependent on other ecclesiastical authorities, and particularly those in Jerusalem, for his message or his commission as an apostle. It is essential to retrace his steps so that the Galatians are reminded of that and even have a sworn report of whom he actually saw on his two visits to Jerusalem.

Paul does not tell us what he did in Arabia or Damascus or the regions of Syria and Cilicia since his intention is not to present his memoirs but to document his relationship with the Jerusalem apostles. The suggestion has often been made that Arabia represents his retreat, his place of meditation and preparation for the busy years ahead of missionary activity. In numerous sermons Arabia has symbolized the call for spiritual renewal; the call to get away from the hustle and bustle of modern life. That is pure speculation. A better case could be made for his engagement during this time in preaching to the inhabitants of the northern Nabataean kingdom, perhaps in Petra, with the result that his reputation filters north to the Judaean churches (1:22–24). Luther comments, "What else was he to do but preach Christ?" ("Lectures on Galatians—1535," *Luther's Works,* J. Pelikan, ed., Vol. 26, 74). But for either explanation the evidence is skimpy, and interpreters would do well to resist the temptation to imagine what Paul might or should have done in Arabia.

Another reason for the inclusion of the autobiographical material is less obvious but perhaps more crucial to Paul's argument. Paul's own life manifests the power of the gospel. At the heart of his apostleship lies the action of the message which transforms him from the zealous Pharisee who persecutes the church to the preacher to the Gentiles. He takes no credit for the change; his mention of it indicates no egotistical mania. It is the work of God's grace. But it is a fact which neither he nor the Galatians can deny. Even the churches of Judea, who would not recognize Paul if they saw him, hear of the radical reversal and glorify God because of him (1:22–24).

Since subjection to the gospel is primary in determining

27

apostolic authority, mention of the change in his life effected by the gospel is decisive in the Galatian letter. Paul does not rest his case for being heard on an understanding of an apostle as one duly elected to an office and whose authority lies either in the legitimacy of the election or the prominence of the office. Real authority derives from the gospel, and thus the issue for an apostle is his subjection to and manifestation of that gospel.

3. What is to be made of the statement that Paul received the gospel "through a revelation of Jesus Christ" (1:12)? The sentence suggests at first glance that Paul is pointing to a personal vision he has had in which special information has been conveyed to him and that he will not tolerate challenge or disagreement with what he has learned in the vision. The church has known in its history enough ecstatic visionaries to be wary of those who claim so much for their private theophanies. Is Paul a disruptive mystic who jeopardizes the unity of the church for the sake of his individual experience? Furthermore, how are verses 11–12 to be understood in light of I Cor. 15:3, where Paul clearly refers to a specific statement about Christ which he received from those who were Christians before him and which he in turn transmits to the Corinthians?

Two things can be said which throw light on the issue, if indeed they do not provide an answer. First, though the word "revelation" in Paul can refer to a particular disclosure made to an individual in a mystical or charismatic sense (cf. I Cor. 14:6, 26, 30; II Cor. 12:1, 7), it can also describe the unveiling of a reality hidden from the world but made known to others by the activity of the Spirit (cf. I Cor. 2:6ff; Rom. 16:25; Eph. 3:3, 5). In such cases the revelation has to do with some facet of God's redemptive purpose. It is in this latter sense that Paul intends the word here. There is no hint that in the revelation he receives new information that no one else has—like Joseph Smith who discovers from an angel in 1827 plates for the Book of Mormon. Simply, the veil which has hidden God's Son from him is removed and Paul sees him.

Secondly, Paul does not thoroughly equate "gospel" with the tradition containing the historical and interpretive statement about Christ's death and resurrection. One can hear the recitation of the tradition and not be gripped by the gospel. The gospel, as we have seen, is primarily a divine power whereby God changes people and situations. Of course it has content, and that content can be expressed in terms of the tradition, as

28

in I Cor. 15:3ff, but the tradition does not exhaust the meaning of "gospel." When Paul says, "I did not receive it from man, nor was I taught it, but it came through a revelation of Jesus Christ," he is speaking of "gospel," not merely information about Jesus Christ. Undoubtedly he knew something about the death and the resurrection of Jesus before his Damascus Road experience, else he would not have bothered to persecute the church. It seems hardly possible that when Paul went to Jerusalem and stayed with Peter for fifteen days they refused to talk about theological matters of serious consequence. The infinitive in 1:18 translated in the RSV as "to visit" actually means "to get to know someone" or "to get information from someone." But knowledge of the tradition is not the same as the experience of God's revealing his Son "to me" (1:16). What distinguishes the gospel is that it comes "not only in word, but also in power and in the Holy Spirit, and with full conviction" (I Thess. 1:5).

Though there is clearly a difference of emphasis due to the particular contexts, no fundamental contradiction exists between Gal. 1:11–12 and I Cor. 15:3. Paul in Galatians does not denigrate the early Christian tradition regarding Jesus' death and resurrection. He obviously received it himself and passed it on, as I Cor. 15:3 says. When the question of authority arises, however, Paul turns not to tradition (at least tradition *qua* tradition) but to gospel and thus to the moment in his own pilgrimage when he discovered it as good news. That did not happen as the result of any individual's influence on his life, but as "a revelation of Jesus Christ." Or to state it another way, Paul's secondary concern in Galatians is *how* the gospel was received (by tradition or immediate revelation); his primary concern is *from whom* it came (from other humans or God). If he believes, as he clearly does, that the gospel authenticates his activity and authority as an apostle, it is not surprising that the divine source of the gospel should be a repeated emphasis in his argument.

Galatians 1:15–16
Paul's Call

29

After the resurrection of Jesus, no single event affected the course of the church's history so much as did the call of Paul.

Other individuals were converted; Constantine even baptized an empire. But the change which occurred for Paul caused reverberations, many of which are still resounding in the church (e.g., his revolutionary insight, if no more than an insight, in regard to the place of women, in 3:28). Not only is there the deposit of his letters in the New Testament canon with their subsequent influence in later history, there is also the bold mission to Greece and the west, which, while not solely Paul's doing, nevertheless opened new frontiers for the expansion of Christianity.

Paul's call is also an important topic for preaching and teaching and worth detailed consideration here. It has often been a misunderstood experience, interpreted in light of the personal history of the interpreter or in light of a traditional understanding of what a conversion *ought* to be or in light of the insights of one or another school of psychology. The various interpretive keys have led to descriptions of a conversion—only not Paul's. And thus it is necessary to look carefully at Paul's own description and interpretation of the experience.

First a word about sources. Gal. 1:11–16; Phil. 3:4–11; I Cor. 15:8–11 provide the fullest interpretations from Paul himself (with scattered references in passages like I Cor. 9:1; II Cor. 4:6). Since they come from undisputed Pauline letters, these references obviously carry the most significance. The three accounts recorded by Luke (Acts 9:1–9; 22:3–16; 26:9–18) are incorporated into the purpose and theology of Acts and can serve only as secondary sources. They contain discrepancies in details from Paul's own report (e.g., the role of Ananias in the Acts accounts in contrast to Gal. 1:16c), and yet share in common the primary import of the experience.

In light of the texts themselves, several words of caution about contemporary interpretations of Paul's call are appropriate. First, what happened on the Damascus Road was a unique experience, Paul's own, and we need to be wary of taking it as a model conversion after which all others should be patterned. "From Saul to Paul" is a convenient slogan to use in talking about the need for radical change in the lives of individuals, but Paul never sets up his experience as a prototype to be followed by others. For example, a crucial feature of his account in Galatians is the statement that following God's revelation to him he "did not stop to discuss this with any human being" (1:16c, Jerusalem Bible), hardly wise counsel for the typical new convert. The task of interpreting the Damascus Road experience

30

today is not to hunt for the universal elements which should be in every conversion experience, but rather to learn from Paul's account of his own experience something of the nature of the gospel.

Secondly, not only do we need to be wary of using Paul as a pattern for contemporary experiences, we need to be wary of using contemporary experiences to interpret Paul. As has been frequently noted, Martin Luther fell precisely into this trap. His own search for self-justification as an Augustinian monk and his abrupt change led him to identify with Paul and to derive from Paul's accounts conclusions based on his own experiences. Luther's life before his discovery of justification by faith was marked by periods of depression and intense anxiety because he feared that he had not done enough to atone for his sin. To learn of God's gracious justification was to receive free forgiveness and the release of an enormous burden of guilt. And he interpreted Paul's experience in like manner. The only problem is that Paul never indicates that he was laden with guilt or frustrated by his unsuccessful efforts to win God's approval prior to Damascus Road. On the contrary, Paul testifies that he made remarkable advances in his religious development, was blameless as regards righteousness under the law, and out of deep convictions persecuted the church which he felt was blasphemous. There is no hint (except in a strained exegesis of Rom. 7:7–25) that Paul had a tortured conscience and troubled soul which Christ then replaced with peace of mind and eternal security. Luther's interpretation (or misinterpretation) of Paul's change colored his view of the doctrine of justification and of course exerted tremendous influence on later interpreters, a point to which we shall return later.

The same fallacy of reading into Paul the experience of another has also shaped certain pietistic interpretations. The change from a life of irresponsibility or waywardness to moral zeal and stability, which may have been the experience of the interpreter, becomes the pattern of Paul's change (as if he had been the prodigal son coming home from the bars and brothels of the far country). And often the accompanying statement of God's justifying act in Christ suggests that God's primary concern is that we be more moral or religious, certainly not the central issue for Paul.

Thirdly, we need to be wary of psychologizing Paul's experience, that is, of interpreting the incident itself or its dramatic sequel in terms of the insights of modern psychology or psychia-

31

try. The problem here is that the sources do not lend themselves to such an interpretation. Paul does not really let the
reader into his inner life so that one can grasp the dynamics at
work in his personality. To be sure, there are interesting details
in Paul's life about which one could speculate—the strange
reference to the way he became a Christian (I Cor. 15:8), his
attitude about his achievements and his heritage (Phil. 3:4–8),
the sudden about-face—but they subserve a theological rather
than a biographical purpose. Any psychological explanation of
Paul's conversion would have to be based on considerable conjecture. This is not to suggest, however, that the insights of
psychology cannot be helpful in interpreting today the meaning of the same grace Paul experienced at Damascus Road. But
that is another matter.

With primary attention to Gal. 1:12–16 and occasional
glances at the other sources, what can be said about this experience?

1. It represents a critical moment in the history of God's
working in Paul's life. He refers to the incident in his letters not
by describing the outward details (the light, the voice, his companions) nor by what he felt at the time (elation, relief, security),
but by what God was doing in his life. All in one (frightful!)
subordinate clause, he writes, "But when he who had set me
apart before I was born, and had called me through his grace,
was pleased to reveal his Son to me, in order that I might preach
him among the Gentiles . . ." (1:15–16b). The experience was
in fact not the first time God, the Father of Jesus Christ, had had
to do with him. Before his birth he had been chosen for a task.
Those hours of study under Gamaliel, the enthusiasm he
showed in keeping the details of the law, the commitment
which led him even to root out the blasphemous Christians had
not happened outside the eye of a gracious God. And then God
decided it was the right moment and "revealed his Son to me."
What occurred was an event which from Paul's theological way
of evaluating it was a crucial step in God's long-term activity
with him. It was not his decision to become an apostle, a
preacher among the Gentiles; it was God's decision. It was
God's voice which called him, God's hand which grasped him,
God's grace which opened his eyes to see his Son.

32   But what does it really mean to live as one so called and
grasped? Two things at least are worth noting. First, it means
that life has direction and purpose. Events which seem random
and fortuitous are ultimately oriented toward a goal and thus

make sense. They are pieces of a puzzle which in turn fits together with numberless other puzzles to comprise a huge mosaic. Certainly this is an affirmation of faith and not a statement which can be verified by scientific or historical procedure. Neither the small puzzle nor the large mosaic can be seen from our vantage point in time and history. Likewise, this affirmation of faith is not to be used as an easy explanation of human tragedy and pain, to cheer up a sufferer or to silence the cries of the grieving. For many there remain moments which often stretch into long periods where life seems rude, senseless, and indiscriminate; and the casual, detached counsel of "Christian friends" sounds no better than the words of Job's comforters. (Often it is the friends' way of protecting themselves against pain.) But that is not the whole story. The God who calls and grasps us is the Father of Jesus Christ, both crucified and risen. He was neither casual nor detached on Good Friday. Human sufferings, then, can be faced in the light of Easter toward which Jesus moved in the time of his great suffering.

Secondly, the reality of being called and grasped provides enormous support for getting about one's task. In moments of crisis people have the remarkable capacity to second-guess themselves. "Should I have taken this option? What if I had done differently?" Doubting one's course of action seems inevitable at one time or another. Choices have to be made, many clouded by uncertainty and confusion. But self-doubts become paralyzing, particularly in the face of possible failure. The solution lies not in dogged self-reliance ("I can master this situation") or in resigned compliance ("Somehow I'll muddle through"), but in the conviction that one is called, called in the first place not to be a salesperson or a surgeon or a soldier but to be a Christian (and that means, as it did for Paul, of course a Christian witness). The decision as to what one is ultimately about in life, that is, being a Christian, is not one's own to be fretted over; it is God's decision. That takes a burden off and opens up incredible resources for coping with life and its problems (Phil. 4:19). It enables one to be amazingly optimistic in dark hours, even light-hearted about momentous tasks, certainly with a sense of humor about oneself.

2. Paul's conversion and his commission to preach the gospel are not two separate events; they are one. In a single subordinate clause Paul can include God's electing him, calling him, revealing his Son to him, and sending him to the Gentiles. It is not a two-step process: as a first step God saves him and then,

33

after sufficient maturity, as a second step God gives him a task. For this reason, it is more accurate to describe what happened on the Damascus Road with a broader term like "call" (including both conversion and commission) rather than with the more usual "conversion." The accounts in Acts as well as the other references in Paul's letters concur with this.

Paul underscores this himself when, describing his experience, he employs the language of the summons of the Old Testament prophets. He particularly reflects Jeremiah's call, "Before I formed you in the womb I knew you, and before you were born I consecrated you; I appointed you a prophet to the nations" (Jer. 1:5), and probably alludes also to the calling of the suffering servant of Second Isaiah (49:1, 5–6). Both these Old Testament passages have more to do with the gracious election of the chosen and the assignment given him than with a conversion from one state to another.

There is something to be learned about the nature of the faith from the way Paul unites conversion and commission into a single event. What does it mean concretely and practically to be a Christian? That is a question Karl Barth addresses in an illuminating section of his *Church Dogmatics* (IV/3, pp. 554–614). The classic answer, Barth suggests, is to point to the benefits of Christ. The Christian is one "who is distinguished from others by the address, reception, possession, use, and enjoyment of the salvation of God given and revealed to the world by God in Jesus Christ" (p. 561). The Christian is a recipient of grace and thus experiences the reconciliation, forgiveness, joy, peace and hope to be found in Christ. Many hymns sung in our churches enumerate the benefits for us; the benefits have certainly been popular themes for sermons. The trouble with this classic answer is that it is fraught with the temptation to assume that the enjoyment of God's gifts constitutes the only relevant and important reality to which God calls people. *My* salvation, *my* peace of mind, *my* assurance of God's blessing (or perhaps in other circles, *my* self-actualization, the fulfillment of *my* potential as a person, doing *my* thing) become exclusive concerns. Christ, the Lord at whose disposal Christians put themselves, becomes a genie to supply at a beck and call personal blessings.

34

It gives us a very strange relationship if on the one side we have the selflessness and self-giving of God and Jesus Christ, in which the salvation of the world is effected and revealed, and on the other the satisfaction with which Christians accept this and are content to make use of the very different being and action of their Lord (p. 567).

A more biblical answer to the question, What does it mean to be a Christian? is, Barth argues, in terms of the task of being a Christian witness, that is, of being one who in word and deed points to God and to what he has been doing, is doing, and will be doing in relation to the world. Rather than a preoccupation with the good gifts God bestows on the individual Christian, the primary center around which life is oriented is the spoken word and the service of love rendered the world. Barth finds conclusive support for his answer in the various calls of biblical characters. Certainly Paul's experience is a confirmation. None of the accounts mentions his newly found joy, peace, or security immediately resulting from Christ's revelation to him; instead the accounts point to the mission to which he was being directed (". . . in order that I might preach him among the Gentiles"). At the core of the Christian experience a centrifugal force pushes believers—sometimes successfully, sometimes not—beyond the temptation to tarry forever with their own problems or with the preoccupation with Christ's benefits so that they may join God's work in convincing the world of his holy love.

3. The converted and commissioned Paul bears features of both continuity and discontinuity with the Saul of Pharisaic zeal. While our immediate concern is with the changes, the new understandings which happen as a part of his experience, it is essential to note that lines of continuity reach back to his days prior to his conversion. Paul was no Marcionite. The God who had revealed himself in the face of Jesus Christ was the God of Israel who had spoken to Abraham in anticipation of what would transpire (3:8) and had called Paul before his birth (1:15). "The law and the prophets" (which Christians call the Old Testament) remain for Paul holy scripture, though read in a new light. Israel retains specific prerogatives as the chosen people of God (cf. Rom. 9:4–5), and Paul continues to regard himself as a *Jewish* Christian (cf. the predominant way he uses the pronoun "we," e.g., 2:15). Though Paul aggressively counters those who insist that Gentiles must become Jews in order to be complete Christians, he himself never ceases to be a Jew.

Changes in Paul do occur. We shall mention from the accounts of his call the two most critical.

(a) At the center undoubtedly is Paul's new understanding of Christ. God "was pleased to reveal his Son to me" (1:16; I Cor.

35

9:1; 15:8; II Cor. 4:6). One reason why Paul had reacted as vigorously as he did in opposition to the first Christians was their incomprehensible message about a crucified Messiah. How could they preach that a person, admittedly cursed by the law as seen by the manner of his death (3:13; Deut. 21:23), had been raised by God from the dead? Such a message to a Jew is offensive (I Cor. 1:23)—until one is grasped by that Christ and discovers that he has been established Son of God in power (Rom. 1:3–4). Then everything previously cherished is set aside for "the surpassing worth of knowing Christ Jesus my Lord" (Phil. 3:8).

This point is not one Paul would relegate to a concluding paragraph in an article entitled "How I Changed My Mind." In fact, it is not an academic point at all but a revolutionary reality which re-orients life and puts people like Paul going in the opposite direction. It has to do with how God sets persons and things right in the world, not through a vigilant keeping of the law but in Christ who can be related to only on the grounds of faith. To be grasped by Christ is to discover a whole new world where standards of success once dearly held no longer matter, where criteria for decisions are radically altered, where people are viewed in a different light (cf. II Cor. 5:14–17, NEB).

(b) Closely related to Paul's changed view of Christ is his view of the people of God. As a Pharisee it was impossible for him to entertain the notion that God had acted toward the early Christians in the way they claimed. It was outrageous to consider that the Messiah had been revealed to people who were at best religiously marginal, who lacked sufficient piety and commitment to the law, and who could be looked on with contempt. Paul's conviction was abruptly reversed, however, and he found himself engaged in a mission not merely to the nominally religious Jews but to Gentiles who stood completely outside the pale of the law. The dialogue in the Acts account (9:4–6) calls attention to this new perspective. "Saul, Saul, why do you persecute me?" "Who are you, Lord?" "I am Jesus, whom you are persecuting." The Lord is identified as Jesus, and Jesus is described as the one who has bound himself to this contemptible community Paul is seeking to eliminate. This identification throws a different light on the nature of the people of God. God is the one "who justifies the ungodly" (Rom. 4:5), and his people are none other than the ungodly whom he justifies.

No wonder, then, that Paul describes his call in the lan-

36

guage of Jeremiah's call and the call of Isaiah's suffering servant, both of whom were sent "to the nations." No wonder that he turns to Abraham to whom the promise was given, "In you shall all the nations be blessed" (3:8; Gen. 12:3). The people of God are redefined to include people of faith (3:9) rather than those with a specific religious and ethnic heritage. The law as a fence to separate Gentile from Jew is gone. Neither race nor color nor sex nor economic status nor education nor politics plays any part in determining who shares in the community of God. This may sound like a worn-out truism until one discovers that, despite the many sermons on race relations and the activity of numerous councils on human relations, the term "Christian" is still used in today's world to exclude, to segregate, to separate people, like a wall to keep out undesirables. As in the Galatian letter the issue is theological; the message of justification by faith has become justification by being "our kind of people." Thus the universalism Paul struggled for remains today a major challenge to the church.

There are of course other changes in Paul precipitated by the events on the Damascus Road—his way of reading the Old Testament, his awareness of how God sets things right in the world, his understanding of the intention and function of the law. But these are issues that emerge in other passages in the epistle and thus are commented upon elsewhere.

Galatians 2:1–10
The Search for Unity

The particular incident recorded in 2:1–10 has attracted a great deal of interest through the years from historians seeking to trace the development of the early church and how it coped with its major problem of including Gentiles in a community which was initially Jewish. Where does this visit to Jerusalem fit into the sequence of Paul's visits mentioned in Acts, or does it fit? If this visit parallels one of those found in Acts, has Paul or Luke slanted the record of the meeting to a particular purpose? Did a struggle for power between Jerusalem and Antioch lie behind this meeting, and if so, how was it resolved? These (among others) are important questions to ask in seeking to understand how a small group of Jewish followers in Jerusalem

37

at the time of Jesus' resurrection came to be a predominantly Gentile movement at the end of the century with congregations scattered around the Mediterranean world. Our concern here, however, is a slightly different and in a sense more modest one. Given the incident as recorded (2:1–10), what function does it perform in the argument of the epistle? What is Paul saying to the Galatians in terms of their immediate problems? What can the church learn from this passage about its own identity and vocation? The two sets of questions—those of the historian and those of the theologian—are not unrelated and certainly impinge on each other. Neither interpreter can afford to ignore the other. But the reasons for investigating the text invariably lead the two in slightly different directions.

The passage is a part of the autobiographical section (1:11—2:21) in which Paul records for the Galatians his relations with the Jerusalem church. His purpose, in line with the thrust of chapter one, is to assure his readers that his reception of the gospel cannot be traced to another human source or influence but only to the activity of the risen Christ. This, then, is his second trip to Jerusalem since his call; and he explains that in his meeting with the "pillar apostles," they "added nothing to me" (2:6). In fact, James, Peter, and John, when they heard the message he was preaching among the Gentiles, gave him their blessings. His account of the visit makes it clear that he is not dependent on the Jerusalem authorities for his commission of the message, but that both his commission and his message are recognized and accepted by them.

The fact that the meeting at Jerusalem turned out the way it did enables Paul to use his report of it for still another purpose. The church, though struggling with a Jew-Gentile problem and undoubtedly strained to the breaking point, is nevertheless one church. The Galatian Christians need to hear this and to be reminded of the foundation on which that oneness is built. The agreement reached at this meeting and even the single condition placed on Paul's venture among the Gentiles ("only they would have us remember the poor") provides an excellent occasion for Paul to clarify the unity of the church based on the one gospel of grace. The account of the conflict between Peter and Paul which follows in 2:11–21 sharpens even further this relation between the gospel and the unity of the church.

Structurally, verses 1–10 are divided rather neatly into

three parts. First, verses 1–2 give the reasons for Paul's trip with
Barnabas and Titus to Jerusalem. He was not called on the
carpet by the Jerusalem leaders because of his independent
tendencies, but rather went "by revelation." It is impossible to
determine with certainty what this phrase means. One can only
say that the trip involved laying before the leaders the message
he had been preaching among the Gentiles, "lest somehow I
should be running or had run in vain" (2:2). On the surface, this
suggests that Paul was anxious about his activity and was sub-
mitting himself to the authority of Jerusalem in order to get
confirmation of his mission and message. But such an interpretation contradicts verses 1 and 11–12 and the rest of the letter.
It is more likely that Paul's anxiety stems not from an uncertainty about the gospel but from a fear for the unity of the
church. If James, Peter, and John had rejected Paul's message,
it seems hardly possible that Paul would have desisted in his
efforts to reach the Gentiles or would have accommodated his
preaching to make it anything other than a word of God's grace
in Christ. But he would have been deeply disturbed at their
rejection since it would likely have split the early Christians into
two or more groups, each with its own view of mission. So Paul
goes to Jerusalem with a certain amount of apprehension about
whether the leadership there is really subject to the gospel and
whether the unity of the church can be maintained.

Paul may well have had good reason for being apprehen-
sive about the reaction in Jerusalem to his missionary activity,
if not to his gospel. The view evidently prevailed among the
predominantly Jewish elements of the church that the task of
mission was first to Israel and only after the conversion of the
Jews should attention be given to the Gentiles. After all, when
Jesus commissioned the Twelve, he told them to stay away from
Gentile and Samaritan towns and to concentrate on "the lost
sheep of the house of Israel" (Matt. 10:5–6). Paul, however,
senses the urgency of the present time as the right moment for
a mission to the Gentiles. They will actually become the means
whereby Israel will be saved (Rom. 11:25–26). This very conviction pushes him all the harder for understanding and solidarity
with the Jerusalem leaders. He has no interest in starting a new
and separate cult.

The second part of the pericope (2:3–5) relates the circumstances surrounding the possible circumcision of Titus, Paul's
Gentile companion. Unfortunately the details are not entirely

39

clear due to a problem in the transmission of the Greek text and to the uncertainty as to who the "false brethren" were and where they carried out their spying activities. The latter evidently urge the circumcision of Titus during this visit to Jerusalem but are unable to persuade the Jerusalem leaders to go along with them. Paul includes the incident as part of his record of the visit for two reasons: to show that the "pillar apostles" agree with him and not with the "false brethren" and to make the point that the circumcision of a Gentile under duress violates "the truth of the gospel."

The question is often raised: How can Paul have taken such a decisive position in resisting the circumcision of Titus and yet, according to the Acts tradition (16:3), have arranged for the circumcision of another colleague Timothy? Clearly in both instances the issue is one of freedom. In the case of Timothy, whose mother was Jewish, Paul acts on the basis of the freedom he has in Christ to become as a Jew for the sake of communicating the gospel to Jews (cf. I Cor. 9:19–23). With Titus, however, the situation is different. He is being pressured by the "false brethren," and to yield would be to renounce that very liberty he exercised in connection with Timothy. The two opposite actions Paul takes emerge from his awareness that God has graciously freed humanity from the burden of religious restrictions, including circumcision, and that in freeing humanity he has set it in the service of the gospel of freedom.

The third component of the pericope is 2:6–10. It records the actual meeting with the "pillar apostles," the recognition they give to the source of Paul's authority, the agreement on a common mission with a necessary division of labor, the giving of the right hand of fellowship, and the request to Paul and his companions that they not neglect the poor. The verse beginning the section (2:6) needs clarification since it not only is important in revealing Paul's attitude towards the Jerusalem leaders but is also highly ambiguous. In the Greek text it contains an incomplete sentence which only adds to the ambiguity. The repeated phrase "those who were reputed to be . . ." suggests a negative attitude toward the figures at Jerusalem as if Paul were sneering, at least slightly, at their prominence and place of esteem. David Hay, however, in an important article on the verse, has made a good case for saying that Paul does not disparage James, Peter, and John when he writes, "And from those who were reputed to be something (what they were makes no difference to me; God shows no partiality)—those, I say, who were of repute added nothing to me." He is simply telling the Galatians that decisions about apostles should not be made on external considerations (literally, "God does not receive a person's face"). They should judge by reality (i.e., conformity of message and life to the gospel), not by appearance (i.e., mere rank). For himself, the status of the "pillar apostles" was not so decisive that they could have dissuaded Paul from preaching the message of God's unconditional love for the Gentiles. But happily they did not try to do so. (David Hay, "Paul's Indifference to Authority," *Journal of Biblical Literature* 88:36–44, 1969).

Paul indicates that the meeting ended on a high note of agreement, fellowship, and mutual support. The mention of the poor further underlines the sense of unity, since the reference is to the poor in the church at Jerusalem (cf. Rom. 15:26). Paul, as we know from other letters, worked among the predominantly Gentile congregations to gather a collection for those in the mother church not only to ease their dire plight, but to make tangible the bond which drew diverse groups together in the Christian community. It was a way for Gentiles to acknowledge their indebtedness for the spiritual blessings which belonged to the Jews and to offer a visible expression of the mutual concern they shared in Christ (cf. Rom. 15:27).

Two theological affirmations emerge worthy of further consideration. First, *the unity of the church is built on one gospel of grace.* This means, then, that the common tie drawing Christians together is not to be discovered in mere agreement about doctrinal matters or in a joint ethnic heritage or in a national bond or in social homogeneity. These are matters to which people are naturally attracted and often determine the constituency of a church or congregation in North America, if not in the West generally. The question, however, is whether these particular attractions usurp the function of the gospel as the essential bond of the church and end up as exclusive rather than inclusive ties. Rather than a unity, what tends to develop is a uniformity of perceptions, morals, or styles of life; and those who fail to conform move on or drop out. In contrast, what we learn from verses 1–10 is that the gospel produces a church in which unity exists with amazing diversity. Paul may at times appear to be an extremely stubborn theologian whose dogmaticism is uncompromising, and yet ironically the truth he strug-

41

gles for in the early church is one of diversity and mutuality, where Gentiles are not forced to become Jews and *vice versa*. Being clear about the nature of the gospel does not constrict or confine the church; instead, it removes all the false conditions to unity laid on by years of tradition. A passion for the singularity of the message, when the message is one of grace and forgiveness, issues in an open church in which freedom is not destroyed either by the pressure of conformity or by the contending force of pluralism. It is, to use Moltmann's phrase, "an evangelical unity," not an ethnic, social, or legal one (cf. Jürgen Moltmann, *The Church in the Power of the Spirit,* p. 343).

In the light of the struggles of many modern church groups, it is necessary to distinguish a unity based on the gospel from a unity based on the lowest common denominator. Groups, whether of individuals, congregations, or denominations, often begin their search for reconciliation by looking at the history, the traditions, the liturgy, or the sociological situations of each in order to find somewhere among the past or the present a simple pattern of thought or style of life on which all can agree. When this lowest common denominator is finally uncovered, it becomes the foundation on which to build mutuality. Of course an understanding of the history, traditions, liturgy, and social composition of the other is significant, but for Paul it is not the starting point and certainly not the *sine qua non* of Christian unity.

A second thing to be learned from 2:1–10 is that the *one gospel of grace pushes Christians towards a visible unity.* It must have crossed Paul's mind that he could do without Jerusalem. The further west his missionary travels took him and the more cosmopolitan the Christian community became, the less likely it would be that he would have to worry about whether those in the mother church agreed with him or not. This sort of thinking, however, neglects an imperative at the heart of the gospel. One cannot be an empire-builder or a separatist and at the same time be a passionate advocate of God's free grace. "By revelation" (perhaps meaning the same revelation that occurred on the Damascus Road) Paul was directed to go to Jerusalem and consult with the authorities about the nature of his mission and message.

Elsewhere in Paul (e.g., I Cor. 12:12–26, 27; Rom. 12:4–5; Gal. 3:26–29) we learn that the unity of the church is a given, a spiritual reality bestowed by Christ which joins his people to

42

himself and to each other. But like so many other indicatives in the New Testament, this affirmation stands under an imperative. To be one in Christ means constantly to be alert to those experiences in life and history when the gospel leads to a visible unity between individuals, groups, and churches. Sometimes it happens as a serendipitous moment, the by-product of a common venture. But more often, as with Paul, unity comes only after long and frank conversation in which there is the risk of disagreement. It emerges as two parties struggle persistently to resolve a complex problem or as they dare to confront "false brethren," who want a unity based on faulty premises or no unity at all.

The difficult question is exactly how this push to unity is to be understood in a country like the United States where a bewildering variety of denominations exist, or in other contexts where small and often lively groups operate outside the bounds of a national church. Should all who seek to declare the gospel of Christ necessarily merge into one gigantic organization in spite of fundamental differences of doctrine, worship, and patterns of life? Since Paul was not faced with a situation analogous to the contemporary one, verses 1–10 cannot be made to answer all our modern questions, much as we would like it to. Even to refer to the Jerusalem meeting as an ecumenical council is a bit misleading since there were groups in the early church not represented at the meeting, for example, the Hellenists of Acts 6—7 and Apollos. Still, one cannot dismiss Paul simply as a proponent of an invisible unity which celebrates its oneness in secret. He went physically to Jerusalem with his companions, presented the message he had been preaching, resisted outside pressures to circumcise Titus, struggled through the issues to mutual decision, promised further material support, and reported the whole proceedings in an open letter to the Galatian congregations.

The passage does not answer every modern concern, but it does throw light on the nature of Christian unity.

(a) It is a unity discovered in the context of mission. Paul is not preoccupied here with how to coordinate the bureaucracies of Antioch and Jerusalem so that they can work together more effectively and economically. Organizational needs and problems are real in the modern world in a different way from those in the first century, and precisely for this reason one must be careful not to get the cart before the horse. It is when the

43

church takes its apostolic character seriously that new occasions for experiencing unity occur. The missionary movement of the nineteenth century gave rise to the ecumenical history of the twentieth. Today the so-called younger churches of the developing nations, historically the products of older churches, are increasingly recognized as equal partners who can help the older churches break out of their provinciality and gain a fresh perspective on themselves. The same is true when mission is thought of not in terms of geographical expansion but as the movement of the gospel into unexplored areas of human life and experience. In a curious chain reaction, occasions of visible unity lead to further testimony of the gospel.

(b) It is a unity involving mutuality and participation. The handshake, significantly described as "the right hand of fellowship *(koinonia),*" symbolizes the accord of the meeting. That Peter was "entrusted with the gospel to the circumcised" and Paul "with the gospel to the uncircumcised" did not mean two gospels or even two separate territories of mission but rather a mutual recognition of the work of the other—a viable ecumenical endeavor. In addition, the remembrance of the poor provided at least one occasion after the meeting when Gentile Christians could demonstrate materially their concern for Christian brothers and sisters in Jerusalem.

Christian unity is not to be confused with mere tolerance or indifference or the absence of strife. Like love, it longs for expression in some tangible way, the participation of one partner in the life of the other. Common worship experiences and educational ventures, joint mission projects, the sharing of loaf and cup may not be sufficient, but at least they represent occasions where the celebration of the gospel in word and deed can be a unifying bond and congregations can move a step or two beyond their separateness.

Since the interpretation of this passage has largely dealt with Paul's concern for the oneness of the church, a word needs to be said about the relation of 2:1–10 to the next section (2:11–21), where Paul takes the initiative in confronting Peter publicly over a further issue regarding the Gentiles. It looks as if the unity reached at Jerusalem was short-lived and as if Paul changed his tune and precipitated a major split. Four brief comments are in order. First, the church of the New Testament period should not be idealized as if it were the perfect model

44

to be copied. It was made up of sinful, fallible men and women like the church of every other period, and even its leaders committed serious blunders. Paul certainly thought Peter was in error at Antioch. Secondly, the *practical* issue at stake (2:11–21) is slightly different from that of verses 1–10. There seems to be no question at Antioch about the Gentiles' entrance into the church without circumcision. A further problem, however, emerges. Should Jewish Christians forsake the ceremonial and dietary laws of their tradition in order to eat with Gentile Christians, especially in light of the particular circumstances that prevailed at that moment? Obviously Paul and Peter disagree. Third, we do not know for sure what resulted from Paul's confrontation with Peter. Did it mean a sharp cleavage, or did Peter finally come around to Paul's position? Paul is silent on the outcome. Finally, the *theological* issue at stake in the Antioch confrontation from Paul's perspective is essentially no different from that of the meeting at Jerusalem, that is, the unity of the church must be based on the gospel of grace and nothing else. Thus Paul's action in opposing Peter is not to be understood as a contradiction of the motivation which pushed him to Jerusalem seeking unity; in fact, the two are completely consistent.

Galatians 2:11–21
Contending for the Truth of the Gospel

In approaching this passage the interpreter is faced with its bewildering richness—its blend of narrative and reflection; themes, phrases, and even words heavy with theological import; its enormous resources for teaching and preaching. There are historical problems in Paul's account of his confrontation with Peter, some of which need solution in order to get at the precise point of conflict between the two. Then, in responding to Peter, Paul introduces for the first time in the letter the language of justification and the mutually exclusive choice between "works of the law" and "faith in Christ." But he quickly turns to the theme of dying with Christ in order to expound how it is that one is immune to the law and alive to God. It is not surprising that Luther devoted eighty pages to this peri-

45

cope in his commentary on Galatians—and most of that concentrated on one problem, the relation of law and gospel. The four-fold purpose in this section is a bit more circumscribed. First, it is important to reconstruct the actual dynamics at work in the encounter at Antioch insofar as that is possible. Why did Peter, Barnabas, and the remaining Jewish Christians choose to cease eating with the Gentile Christians? Why did Paul so vigorously oppose that choice? Second, why did Paul include the incident in this letter and at this point in his argument? Third, what can be learned about the structure and logical flow of Paul's rather complicated response to Peter (2:14b–21)? Finally, it is essential to examine the phrases "works of the law" and "faith in Christ" since they play a prominent role in the passage and are of special interest to a theological interpretation. In the section of the commentary which immediately follows this one, detailed consideration will be given to two dimensions of Paul's understanding of justification by faith which have received special attention in recent years and are due particular consideration in teaching and preaching. Such consideration will provide the occasion to relate the themes of justification by faith and Christian unity.

1. The setting is Antioch, where for some time Gentiles had been welcomed into the church, even to the point of sharing common meals with Jewish Christians. (Some commentators say these were meals at which the Lord's Supper was celebrated, though there is nothing decisive in the text to prove that.) Presumably, up to this time there had been no divisive debate in Antioch over the practice of eating together, a habit which clearly ignored the usual categories of Jew and Gentile. When Peter, on his journeys, came to Antioch, he joined in with the Christian community and enjoyed the table-fellowship. Then "certain men from James" arrived and either their presence or the message they brought caused Peter to cease attending the common meals. His withdrawal was so obvious and prominent that Barnabas and the other Jewish Christians were persuaded by his action and likewise absented themselves from table-fellowship with the Gentiles. Paul viewed all this as a failure to be "straightforward about the truth of the gospel" and so confronted Peter publicly. "If you, a Jew, live like a Gentile and not like a Jew in attending the common meals, how can you now forsake these Gentile Christians and compel them to become Jews in order to continue their associations with you?" (2:14, paraphrased).

From the vantage point of a twentieth century Gentile, Peter's decision seems an extraordinary thing, horribly bigoted and provincial, until we examine more closely the details of the narrative (which evidently was a bit less obscure to the original readers). Who were the "certain men" who "came from James"? Who were "the advocates of circumcision"? (2:12, NEB) whom Peter feared so greatly? Admittedly, commentators do not agree on the answers. Some would say the two groups are really the same and that Peter is intimidated by a militant band of Jewish Christians probably connected to the agitators in Galatia. Others argue that the envoys from James are no more than spokesmen for a circumcision party in the Jerusalem church which is irritated that Peter has ceased observing the dietary and ceremonial regulations of his heritage. He is not acting like the missionary to the circumcised (2:9)!

A third explanation (and the most plausible in light of the total picture of the early church) takes account of the intense nationalism of the Jews in Judea at this time. "The advocates of circumcision" (confusingly translated by the RSV as "the circumcision party"), whom Peter fears, are not members of the church at all but zealous Jews who are pressuring the Jewish Christians in Jerusalem to refrain from all associations with Gentiles. Word has reached Jerusalem of Peter's liberal behavior at Antioch, and so James sends emissaries to inform him of the possible repercussions for his Christian brothers and sisters in Jerusalem. In effect, Peter's practice of eating with non-Jews in Antioch is making life more difficult for the Jerusalem church, which has a particular problem of coping with the increasing fervor of Jewish nationalists.

If this third explanation is correct, then Peter's decision to withdraw is based on a concern for the unity and peace of the church, at least the unity and peace of the Antioch and Jerusalem congregations. It is better to abandon the common meals than to make life more difficult for the church in Jerusalem. Paul, on the other hand, sees the theological implications differently. Peter's separation from table-fellowship means that the Gentile Christians can only be considered second-class citizens. If they want to eat with Peter and other Jewish Christians, then they will have to get themselves circumcised and become Jews (". . . *compel* the Gentiles to live like Jews," 2:14 italics mine). The unity of the church would then be based on circumcision and law rather than on the gospel of grace. Furthermore, from Paul's vantage point, Peter's action is interpreted as legalism

47

and thus a denial of the fundamental character of grace (cf. 2:15–21). It is unlikely that Peter would have explained his withdrawal from the table as an attempt to be justified by "works of the law," but Paul does. He does so because he sees that Peter (by his actions if not his intentions) is effectively making a stipulation of the law (circumcision) to be a prerequisite for membership in the people of God.

It is important to recognize that the conflict with Peter, as far as Paul is concerned, is essentially a theological one. Paul gives no indication of a power-struggle between warring factions in the early church—Jerusalem on the one side and Paul and the Gentiles on the other. Neither is Paul's report of the incident intended to be a putdown of Peter the chief apostle, evidence that he is no "rock" but a weak, inferior leader. Oscar Cullmann's analysis of the event leaves one with this impression. Peter, he says, withdrew from eating with the Gentiles contrary to his inner convictions. The group from James exercised such a powerful sway over him that he was intimidated into acting against his better judgment. The picture of Peter here, Cullmann argues, is in line with the psychological pattern demonstrable from the Synoptic accounts—the impulsive disciple who over-zealously swears loyalty to his Lord and yet denies him in the hour of danger (*Peter: Disciple, Apostle, Martyr,* pp. 50–53).

The RSV translation of 2:13 tends to support Cullmann's interpretation. "And with him the rest of the Jews acted insincerely, so that even Barnabas was carried away by their insincerity." The words "acted insincerely" and "their insincerity" imply that Paul thinks Peter (together with the rest of the Jewish Christians) is a wishy-washy, deceitful person who feigns to be something he is not and wields enough power to influence Barnabas and the others. The root word behind both expressions is *upokrisis,* which immediately suggests a translation like "hypocrisy," "lack of principle" (NEB), "play-acting" (F. F. Bruce), or "insincerity." This comes from classical Greek texts where the *upokritēs* is the actor who dons the mask and plays the part assigned to him in the drama. In the writings of Hellenistic Judaism, however, *upokrisis* is always used in the negative sense, but rarely to mean "hypocrisy." More often it denotes "apostasy" or "defiance of God." (Ulrich Wilckens in G. Kittel and G. Friedrichs, eds., *Theological Dictionary of the NT,* VIII, 565). This seems the more appropriate notion here

48

since there is no hint that Peter tries to deceive anyone or that he wears a mask to cover a weakness or that he acts in an underhanded fashion to get his point across. It is unlikely that Barnabas would have sided with Peter unless Peter had had a plausible reason for his decision. Something more is at stake for Paul than Peter's allegedly capricious character or fickle behavior. His concern is not that Peter is insincere but that he is *very* sincere and is blind to the full import of his actions.

2. But our concern is not merely with what happened at Antioch but also with what Paul wishes to say to his Galatian readers through this incident. Why does he include it in the epistle, and how does it function at this particular point in his argument? In light of what precedes and what follows this section, three answers can be given. First, though it is certainly not the primary reason for its inclusion, the incident further clarifies Paul's stance in relation to the Jerusalem apostles. Both Peter and James are opposed here in the cause of "the truth of the gospel." Neither possessed by virtue of his office alone sufficient power to dictate what the gospel or its implications should be. Paul had received his commission to preach independently from them and clearly felt no compulsion to comply with their opinions when those opinions were not consistent with the absolute authority over them and him—the one gospel. The Galatians who are being influenced by the agitators need to be reminded of that. They are, in the final analysis, accountable not to church officials but to the God who calls persons into his grace.

Secondly, the report of the incident serves to reiterate a point made in connection with 2:1–10: the gospel alone provides the bond for Christian unity. The action of Peter and Barnabas could certainly be understood as an expression of concern for fellow Christians and perhaps a move intended to ease the plight of the Jerusalem congregation, hard-pressed by zealous nationalists. But Paul could never agree to unity if it necessitated compromising the gospel and that is what this unity would have done. In like manner, those in Galatia who advocate circumcision are essentially proposing something other than the gospel as a basis for inclusion in the people of God. The alternative facing the Gentiles in Galatia is the same alternative faced by the Gentiles at Antioch who had been forsaken by Peter and Barnabas: become a Jew or remain an inferior member of the church (or no member at all). Both lines

49

of appeal, that of the agitators at Galatia and that of Peter at Antioch, deny the fundamental character of God's grace and set a basis for an exclusive rather than an inclusive unity.

Thirdly, the account of the incident provides a transition to the themes of justification by faith and dying with Christ which are dominant in the following chapter. Paul does not stop (2:14) with his rebuke of Peter, but goes on to the more inclusive language ("we") and the more deliberately theological tone of verses 15–21. For our purpose it is unimportant to determine where his quoted words to Peter leave off and his reflections to the Galatians begin. The incident and the reflections need to be considered as pieces of a unified passage, which the RSV does by including verses 11–21 in a single paragraph. Paul responds to both Peter and the Galatians by explaining how persons are related to God and what life in this relationship means. We turn now to examine the train of thought of verses 15–21 in chapter 2.

3. While Gal. 2:15–21 flows immediately from the incident at Antioch, there is a significant change between verses 14 and 15. The "you" singular of verse 14 fits the theme of verses 11–14, where Paul opposes Peter "to his face." The pronouns of verses 15–17, however, change to the first person plural, putting Paul and Peter no longer in a combative stance but on the same side. A paraphrase: "Peter, you and I are Jews by birth and not 'Gentile sinners,' and yet we know that a person never receives God's favorable judgment simply by keeping the obligations of the law but rather through faith in Jesus Christ. We, too, have believed in Jesus Christ so as to receive the divine acquittal through faith in Christ and not through the law's dictates; for, as the Psalm (143:2) says, based on legal observances no person can receive God's favorable judgment" (2:15–16). Two things on which Peter and Paul agree form the basis of Paul's appeal: People need to be acquitted and set in a right relation to God, and that happens only in Jesus Christ. Given Paul's analysis of the Antioch incident, verses 15–16 present sufficient reason for his opposition to Peter's withdrawal.

Paul goes on to raise a question, however, which may in fact have been raised by one or another of his opponents, but which in this context becomes almost ludicrous. "If in our endeavor to receive God's favorable judgment by being in Christ, we (i.e., Paul, Peter, and other Jewish Christians) ourselves break the law and so are found to be sinners, does this then make Christ an agent of sin? Of course not!" (2:17, paraphrased). The absurd-

50

ity of the question lies in the fact that for Paul the tragedy of sin is not measured by infringements of the law but by rejecting Christ and by denying the meaning of his death as the saving act of God. If one clings to the law as an ultimate standard, then Christians do turn out to be sinners. But Paul can no longer accept this legalistic definition of sin. "If I build up again those things which I tore down, *then* I prove myself a transgressor" (2:18). A reversion to seeking a right relationship to God by means of the law makes one truly a sinner (cf. J. A. Ziesler, *The Meaning of Righteousness in Paul,* pp. 172–74).

Christians have died to the law so that they might live to God (cf. Rom. 7:1–6). Something has happened to enable them to break out from under the old dominion with its slavish control and inevitable condemnation and to live for another lord. That "something" of course is crucifixion with Christ, which carries with it Christ's continued presence which makes possible life and service in the new era. The law has no redemptive authority in this new era. What matters is the mutual life shared in and with Christ.

With verse 18 Paul changes pronouns again, this time from "we" to "I." This could suggest that he intends to refer to his personal history, which of course would exclude Peter and others. If so, then crucifixion with Christ and the resulting life in Christ is being described as the experience of a single individual, perhaps mystical in character. Thus Jesus' death becomes a model which the Christian emulates in his own life. The passage would properly be interpreted in pietistic or existentialist categories. More likely, however, the change in pronouns is stylistic, and the "I" is universal (as in Rom. 7:7–21; I Cor. 6:12–15; 13:1–3, 11–12; etc.). The first person is intended to be inclusive, not exclusive. Paul shows in other places that he understands death and resurrection with Christ as a corporate experience (e.g., Rom. 6:3–8), and it seems unlikely here that he is putting himself at center-stage in the argument. What he affirms is that the death of Christ has happened at a datable point in history but that believers are included in that event with him. They continue to live as recognizable humans in a sinful world, but in the service and power of a risen Lord and in an existence formed by his crucifixion. We shall return later to the implications of this new life.

51

Paul's train of thought through this section is, unquestionably, difficult to follow as he moves from narrative to the forensic language of justification to the idiom of incorporation into Christ. For this reason it is essential to see verses 19–21 as the climax of the argument. Incorporation into Christ and his death explains the radical break with life in the old dominion under the law. It also explains why it is that faith in Christ constitutes a mutually exclusive alternative to works of the law. Christ's death (and believers with him) alone makes the new life a reality (cf. 1:4). Any suggestion on the part of Peter and Barnabas at Antioch or the agitators at Galatia that circumcision or some other demand of the law plays the slightest part in the emancipation proclamation God makes is a repudiation of his grace and a denial of Christ's crucifixion (2:21).

4. Paul sets before his readers a pair of alternatives (2:15–16), which by their repetition tend to dominate this portion of the passage: "works of the law" or "faith in Christ." Though Peter and Paul dispute the practice of Jews and Gentiles sharing common meals, they agree (at least this is the logical explanation of Paul's use of "we") that God's favorable judgment is to be received by trusting Christ, not by observing the precepts of the law. But what does Paul mean by these alternatives, and how are they to be translated for a contemporary age that often defines "faith" as the acceptance of propositions with dubious attestation and "law" as an easily manipulated system used to suppress whoever the enemy happens to be?

(a) The term *law* with its immediate connection to the Hebrew *torah* will be examined in more detail later (in the comments on 3:6–14 and 3:15–29). Here it must be noted that Paul's opposition to "works of the law" rests on his positive conviction that salvation comes exclusively by God's grace in Jesus Christ and from this fact the negative deduction is made that accomplishments of the law can make no contribution to salvation. It is not that Paul is fighting against a group of *avid* legalists; in fact, he accuses his opponents at one point of not observing the law themselves (6:13). Nor is Paul himself against works as such; he later speaks of "faith working through love" (5:6). Presumably the visible deeds done in faith could be exactly the same deeds as those done in response to the law. It is just that when a work of the law, like circumcision, is urged on otherwise uncircumcised people to ensure their inclusion in the household of God, then what is the point of Christ's death? "For if justification were through the law, then Christ died to no purpose" (2:21).

Contemporary "works of the law" may be defined as attitudes or activities which function in such a way as to usurp the grace of God; dispositions, whether religious or not, which aim to accomplish what the death of Christ accomplished. Illustrative are those individuals who set out to carve their own niches in life and who feel that by their personal achievements they can effect a relationship with God and inner peace for themselves. They live with the illusion, conscious or not, that God is to be won over from an antagonistic position. Contemporary novels and dramas, not to mention real life, provide painful examples of driven but unfulfilled people who anticipate the solution to life just beyond the next accomplishment. In effect, salvation by works is an insidious form of idolatry. Its exponents refuse to acknowledge God as the true source of life, but instead turn themselves into gods, dispensers of salvation.

(b) In contrast to "works of the law" Paul sets "faith in Christ," or is it the "faith of Christ"? The RSV, together with the vast majority of recent translations, reads the former; the KJV, almost alone, gives the latter. A very plausible and persuasive case, however, can be made for taking "Christ," which in Greek appears in the genitive case, to be the subject ("Christ's faith" or "Christ's faithfulness") rather than the object ("faith in Christ") of faith. In the instance of the subjective genitive (KJV), what Paul would be contrasting with "works of the law" is not another human reaction, that is, believing in Christ, but an action of Christ himself, his unflinching faithfulness to the will of God, his obedience unto death even in the face of godforsakenness. This is supported by the Old Testament concept of faith, which carries a heavy stress on fidelity, loyalty, and faithfulness. These two instances of the phrase in verse 16 are not the only occasions where this phrase occurs in Pauline literature. A final decision as to which translation is to be preferred must take into account a number of complex factors and parallel passages, which to investigate here would involve too lengthy a discussion. (For a clearly stated argument in favor of the KJV translation, see George Howard, *Paul: Crisis in Galatia*, pp. 95–96 and the other articles cited there.)

If "faith of Christ" is the translation, the effect is to highlight the christological focus of justification, yet without eliminating the need for a human response of faith (since the verbal form, "we have believed," is unambiguous). The "one who loved me and gave himself for me" obeys his Father without

53

fail, and thus is God's declaration of grace that frees humanity
from the law and its impossible implications that people are to
save themselves (cf. Rom. 5:19). On the other hand, if "faith in
Christ" is the translation, the effect is to stress the element of
human response, yet without eliminating the christological dimension (which otherwise comes in 2:17, 19–21).

Whichever translation is chosen, we still need to examine
more closely the nature of faith as the human response to God's
gracious deed. Perhaps the first thing to observe is that Paul
never does what is being done here. He never analyzes faith or
describes it in any great detail the way he does "love" in the
thirteenth chapter of First Corinthians. An Old Testament
figure like Abraham may be used, in a sense, as a model of faith,
as in Galatians 3 or Romans 4; but even then Paul is interested
primarily in Abraham's place in God's redemptive purposes,
not in a detailed examination of the ingredients which comprise
the human experience of believing. The fundamental character
of faith is that of confession. It draws its meaning completely
from the one confessed—Jesus Christ; and it is Christ with
whom Paul is primarily concerned. But a great deal of confusion
exists about the meaning of faith today and a few comments are
in order.

First, three dangers. Faith is never intended to be a possession people can have to guarantee their status, like a membership card or even a birth certificate. It is God's gift which must
be constantly reappropriated. Thus despite all human efforts to
the contrary, it cannot be mastered, controlled, or manipulated.
There is no way to claim it so as to put God in debt, as if
God owes a special blessing or peculiar care to those who
believe.

Furthermore, since faith is mentioned so frequently in opposition to works of the law, the temptation must be resisted to
turn faith into a work. The line is thin but terribly important
which separates faith as a necessary response to God's grace
from faith as a precondition to grace. Paul regularly uses the
Greek preposition *dia* with the genitive case to mean
"through" faith; he never uses *dia* with the accusative case
which would mean "on account of" faith. Faith is not the ultimate form of self-justification which finally succeeds. Efforts
which seek to refute the doctrine of universalism by insisting on
the necessity of believing in Christ often run the risk of making
faith, like circumcision, something persons perform in order to

54

activate God's otherwise latent justification. But grace with strings attached is no grace at all.

Thirdly, true faith has about it the character of humility, the acknowledgment that one cannot perform deeds which in any way contribute to one's salvation. To be justified by Christ is to be freed from the burden of self-righteousness. All well and good. But continuous rejoicing in one's passivity often turns the publican into the Pharisee. "Thank God I am not like these compulsive do-gooders who feel compelled to help the poor and are always out to change the world. It's a shame they don't know that their good deeds won't save them." Faith is not a reliance on one's accomplishments or *one's lack of accomplishments,* but a trust in the accomplishments of God.

Positively, faith in Christ is the offering of a glad word of thanksgiving for God's goodness focused in the gift of his Son. It is the standing ovation we give when we have caught only a fleeting glimpse of or have been thoroughly gripped by the drama of Good Friday and Easter. With people crowded row on row in front and behind we find ourselves a part of an audience on its feet with applause, whistles, and shouts of "Bravo!" Then in a strange way, almost as if in a dream, we are transformed from isolated spectators into a company of participants, no longer looking on but actually on stage. A moment comes when, moving about from scene to scene, we realize that we are not intruders in someone else's play. We belong here. This is our place, our part. The cross and the resurrection are not only Jesus' but also ours. Faith becomes obedience—not the superficial, formalized adherence to the demands of the law, but conformity to the prime figure in the drama, following him about as he moves among the mass of humanity declaring good news to the poor and release to the captives, binding the brokenhearted, giving garlands instead of ashes, and above all announcing the year of the Lord's favor.

While there is a distinctively personal dimension to faith, it is never marked by isolation or separateness. The *Heidelberg Catechism,* a sixteenth century document noted for its warmth and almost intimate style, provides a beautiful blend of the corporate and the individual dimensions. In answer to the question, "What is true faith?" one reciting the *Catechism* replies:

55

It is not only a certain knowledge by which *I accept* as true all that God has revealed *to us* in his Word, but also a wholehearted trust which the Holy Spirit creates *in me* through the gospel, *that not only to others, but to me also* God has given the forgiveness of sins, everlasting righteousness, and salvation, out of sheer grace solely for the sake of Christ's saving work (italics mine).

Galatians 2:15–21
Justification by Faith

The section 2:15–21 introduces for the first time in Galatians the language of justification by faith and represents one of those texts highly influential on the Protestant reformers of the sixteenth century. Not only contemporary Protestants but also Roman Catholics have been affected by the reformers' struggles with Paul and in particular with his letters to Rome and Galatia. Luther's *sola fide* became a slogan repeated time and again in the preaching and theology of the Protestant church and a watchword against any threat of legalism or unwarranted ecclesiastical control. The confessional documents of the church from the sixteenth century until the present are further witness to the prominence of the doctrine of justification in the theology of the various communions deriving from the reformers.

Contemporary New Testament studies, however, have called attention to two dimensions of Paul's understanding of justification, both of which appear in Galatians and both of which have been neglected from time to time by various streams of Protestant tradition. Each has theological significance for the church's life and thought.

1. Paul's statements on justification arise out of his reflection on and defense of the Gentiles' entrance into the church, not out of his reflection on the question of how personal guilt is alleviated. Krister Stendahl and Markus Barth, among others, have repeatedly pointed out that the church from the end of the first century until the time of Augustine gave almost no attention to Paul's doctrine of justification, because there were no serious debates about the relation of Jews and Gentiles in the church during that period. Augustine, however, in his study of Paul found justification to be the key to his theology. In "making it relevant" he lifted it out of its original context in the missionary struggles of the apostolic period and made it answer the

56

question of guilt raised by the introspective conscience of the typical Westerner. In doing so, Augustine individualized the concept (cf. K. Stendahl, *Paul Among Jews and Gentiles;* and two articles by M. Barth, "The Kerygma of Galatians," *Interpretation* 21:131–46 and "Jews and Gentiles: The Social Character of Justification in Paul," *Journal of Ecumenical Studies* 5:241–67).

The same occurs with Luther. Set against the background of the Medieval casuistic system, his theology was shaped by his personal experience, the absorbing search for relief from guilt, and the burden of worthlessness. The essential question was, How can I, a sinful person, find acceptance in the eyes of a holy and righteous God? The answer came from Paul and particularly from the way Paul understood Habakkuk's words, "He who through faith is righteous shall live." The gracious character of God's deed in Christ, with the realization that this was "for me," produced an experience of freedom and joy. To be sure, Luther did not imagine he was the only soul whom God had justified by faith, but in effect all the rest were simply other cases like his own. They, too, experienced the foolishness of their self-righteousness and heard the divine words of pardon —but for themselves alone. It was, as Luther called it, "the inward way" of justification, "when a person despairs of his former righteousness . . . casts himself down before God, sobs humbly, and confessing that he is a sinner, says with the publican: 'God, be merciful to me a sinner!'" ("Lectures on Galatians 1519," *Luther's Works,* Vol. 27, p. 220). There is no hint in Luther that one's fellow human beings have any part in the event of justification. It is unnecessary to review the whole history of the doctrine since the sixteenth century, but certainly one tendency in Protestantism (and the few exceptions prove the rule) has been to become preoccupied with the individual experience of grace and to articulate the doctrine of justification (and also sanctification) biographically and psychologically.

In light of this history, several features of verses 11–21 need to be underlined. The context is a social setting. The specific point Paul wants to make in that context is that God's favorable judgment in Christ means by its very nature that Gentiles are included in the Christian community on no different level or no different terms than Jews. Both belong at the same table. To put it in negative terms, treating Gentiles as second-class citizens by withdrawing from the common meals is a form of justification

57

by works and thus a denial of the gospel. What Peter fails to recognize at Antioch is that Jews can be justified only together with Gentiles.

Acceptance of God's "not guilty" verdict means acceptance of people with a different history, a different story to tell. God's judgment is corporate ("for us") and only in that context can it also be personal ("for me"). His justifying grace may then appear offensive not only in that it totally disregards human merit but also in that it breaks down otherwise acceptable barriers and brings together radically disparate folks. Such solidarity is not always easy to take. Jonah becomes angry at God's grace in sparing the Ninevites; the elder son refuses to join the family celebration when his prodigal brother returns home; the Pharisee thanks God that he is not like the publican. Still, God's way is to unite as he justifies and justify as he unites. The line in Galatians runs very logically from 2:11–21 to 3:28. "There is neither Jew nor Greek, there is neither slave nor free, there is neither male nor female; for you are all one in Christ Jesus."

While the traditional Protestant understanding of justification was shaped by the effort to answer the guilt and inner tensions of individual consciences, Paul's understanding was shaped by his concern for the Gentiles and his effort to preach Christ in a pluralistic and divided world. With the former, justification includes forgiveness but also takes account of a community of the forgiven who are drawn into a solidarity transcending every possible division.

Repeated reminders of the corporate and social nature of the Christian faith are essential in the modern context where individuals are always on the search for their true individuality. Citizens of the United States are all too familiar with the image of the Lone Ranger derived from an earlier era when settlers pushing West were forced to rely on their own endurance and resourcefulness once they left the more stable environs of the East coast. Individualism and self-reliance came to be basic ingredients in the American myth. The mood is surprisingly unchanged today, though for different reasons. The modern emphasis on individuality results not from a frontier mentality but from coping with a fragmented society. An individual relates to various institutions—home, place of work, church, school, union hall, country club—yet rarely do the institutions have any immediate relationship to each other. How is he or she to get it all together so that life can become more than a collection of bits and pieces? Certainly the Christian faith insists that personal integration never happens as a solo performance.

It is a familiar story. God made a covenant with Israel, yet not with every single soul separately, in isolation from every other soul. At the covenant-making ceremonies, those present and those absent were included; and yet precisely within that covenant relationship individuals discovered true individuality. They were singly addressed by God: "*Thou* shalt have no other gods before me." Their responsibilities bound them inextricably to one another. The story of Achan illustrates how closely a person was bound to his brothers and sisters in Israel. An act of disobedience by one caused distress for the entire nation. The text reads, "For *Achan* . . . took some of the devoted things; and the anger of the LORD burned against *the people of Israel*" (Joshua 7:1).

In the New Testament Christ is the representative person who incorporates in himself the people of God, thus drawing various individuals from their isolation, their self-reliance, their solo performances into a community of faith. At the heart of the community is the judgment of grace which puts all the Lone Rangers on the same level, all dependent on one another in line with their common dependence on the Lord.

2. A second dimension of Paul's understanding of justification noted by recent New Testament scholars is perhaps less neglected than the first, yet more difficult to trace. It basically stems from an incomplete definition of the terms *justify, justification,* and *righteousness,* all of which derive from the same Greek root. It has often been observed that early Protestants and Roman Catholics disputed over the phrase "righteousness of God." Did God only look on believers *as if* they were righteous (which of course they were not), or by an infusion of grace did God actually make them righteous? Granted certain exceptions to the pattern, the Roman Catholic tradition tended to stress righteousness as an effectual gift which so shaped the nature and character of believers that they became truly righteous. The Protestant tradition, on the other hand, was inclined to insist that righteousness was an attribute of God in light of which God makes a judgment in favor of believers, but the believers in themselves remain what they were prior to the judgment. The impasse between the two traditions was due for

59

the most part to the static mode of thinking employed by Medieval theology.

One way out of the dilemma was to look again at the legal-forensic context of justification, particularly in light of its Old Testament roots, and to redefine it in basically relational terms. If the judge renders a favorable verdict, then all the defendants are placed in a new and right relationship to him. Justification has to do with the determination of the relationship, not with a quality inherent in the judge or in those justified. So far so good. What this redefinition, however, fails to emphasize is the divine activity carried on within the established relationship. In giving believers a new relation to himself God does not then abandon them. His gift becomes a power which both obliges them to obey him and makes the obedience possible.

To put this neglected dimension in a traditional way, more attention needs to be paid to the connection between justification and santification in Paul. Often the two have been neatly separated. Justification describes the first stage of salvation, the right relationship to God in which sinful people are initially placed. Sanctification describes the moral and spiritual growth of believers once they are set in the new relationship. Justification demands faith; santification demands obedience. Such a clean split, however, is not supported by Paul.

In verses 15–21 the verb "justify" appears four times. Undoubtedly the forensic-relational dimension of God's action in Christ is intended. The verdict pronounced by the judge in the courtroom is "not guilty." Sinners are set in a right relationship to God. It is a gift and of course has to be received as such—by faith. But the paragraph does not end with verse 17. Paul goes on to speak of the changed situation of the justified. In Christ they have been freed from slavery under the law and now serve a new Lord, whose service is perfect freedom. They have been crucified with Christ and are able to live obediently and faithfully in the new dominion precisely because the new Lord grants his own power to make it possible. In Paul's words, "Christ lives in me."

Ernst Käsemann, who among recent New Testament scholars has called attention to this neglected dimension in the treatment of Paul, comments,

60

The gift [i.e., the righteousness of God] which is being bestowed here is never at any time separable from the Giver. It partakes of the character of power, in so far as God himself enters the arena with it. Thus personal address, obligation, and service are indissolubly bound up with the gift. When God enters the arena, our experience is that he maintains his lordship even in his giving; it is his gifts which are the very means by which he subordinates us to his lordship and makes us responsible beings (*New Testament Questions of Today,* p. 174).

Furthermore, verses 19–20 describe exactly what sort of power God gives in justifying his people. It is found in the experience of being crucified with Christ. Paul significantly uses the perfect tense, "I have been and continue to be crucified with Christ," indicating an action in past time which continues to shape the present. Dying with Christ in this context is not then primarily a reference to baptism, but is rather a description of what it means to live out of and for this new Lord to whom believers are subject. To be sure, the phrase "Christ lives in me" implies a risen figure, but one with the nailprints and wounds very much in evidence. There is no cause for triumphalism or religious flag-waving. Christian existence remains existence "in the flesh," in this human realm where pain, suffering, injustice, and oppression still must be endured and vigorously fought against. At the same time, it is existence "by faith" —taking the leap, rejecting all false offers of security, risking the confession that life can be found in death, and trusting the one "who loved me and gave himself for me." Being crucified with Christ is not a temporary stage to be quickly passed through in the journey toward a blissful life without pain, anguish, and struggle. It remains the daily experience of the community justified and ordered by the power of God.

This was a fitting word for the Galatian situation. The issue under debate, raised by the agitator's demand for circumcision, was basically soteriological, how God saves people. Paul responds by arguing that one must trust God's grace and not rely on human accomplishments. Entrance into Abraham's family comes by hearing and believing, not by birth. But then Paul completely reorients the issue by asserting that salvation is more then simply getting one's name on the list. It has to do with living one's life under the reign of God and of coping with the tension between existence "in the flesh" and existence "by faith." Christ "gave himself for our sins to deliver us from the present evil age" (1:4). To live in the new age into which believers are transferred means to follow the lordship of the self-

61

giving, crucified Christ, to participate in his continuing mission in the world. In other words, justification is not only a gift but also a demand; it is responded to not by a passive resignation but an active obedience.

But what does it mean to live as one who has been crucified with Christ, as one in whom the crucified Christ lives? What does it mean to receive justification not only as a gift but as a power? Here the two neglected aspects of Paul's understanding of justification converge. The righteousness of God—given, received, and lived out—is not just a personal but a corporate reality. It involves participation in a community of people who risk their own security by being *for* others whose histories may be radically different, who culturally, ethnically, economically, politically, and/or socially live on the other side of the tracks. Movement from the old dominion of death to the new dominion of life draws people into a strange fellowship where previously significant divisions no longer matter. To cling to these anachronistic barriers is to reject the demand which the gift of God's righteousness has made. Justification for Paul, then, implies social action in the broadest sense. It implicates the recipient in the cause of sisters and brothers of various circumstances who labor under the weight of oppression, affliction, and personal grief. The divine acquittal is received not by faith which may someday lead to a social concern (or may not) but by faith which *is* social concern, or to use Paul's words, "faith working through love" (5:6).

PART TWO

Faith, Law, and the People of God

GALATIANS 3:1—5:12

In the first two chapters of Galatians Paul addresses the problems of the churches by affirming the authority of the one gospel, which had been received by Jews and Gentiles alike in Galatia and had led them from the present evil age to life in communion and community with Christ. The agitators who had begun after Paul's initial visits to advocate the necessity of circumcision for Gentile converts are opposed in the epistle by the singularity of the gospel. Because the fundamental nature of the gospel is grace, no adjustments or stipulations which suggest it might be conditional can be tolerated. Paul's way of arguing the authority of this gospel is to point to his own history—that he received the gospel from Christ and not from a human source; that it transformed his vocation from being a persecutor of the church to being an apostle to the Gentiles; that at a meeting in Jerusalem the "pillar apostles" hearing his proclamation of it had acknowledged its power. What is more, when Peter by his decision to withdraw from table-fellowship with Gentiles at Antioch in effect denied the gospel, he had to be confronted publicly. The matter of the Gentiles' reception into full participation in the people of God is not one of strategy or politics; it is theological. It concerns the nature of God's actions in the world and what it means to be related to him and to live in that relationship from day to day.

The section which follows chapters one and two (3:1—5:12)

63

represents a change in the style of Paul's approach—from autobiographical reflections to a reminder to the Galatians about their own history and a consideration of Old Testament texts and situations—but no major change in content. It is as if much of 3:1—5:12 is simply an unfolding of the gospel programmatically asserted in Paul's words to Peter (2:15–21), a corollary of what has already been said. He is the exegetical theologian giving careful attention to texts and in one instance drawing a precise distinction because a particular word in the Old Testament appears in the singular rather than the plural (3:16). Still, his intense expressions of pastoral concern for the Galatians interspersed throughout the section (4:8–11, 12–20; 5:2–12) remind the reader that the network of Old Testament citations is not dispassionate or unrelated. There are real people in Galatia who need help in re-thinking their commitments to the Christian faith. At times Paul is pessimistic (4:11), at times optimistic (5:10), about the outcome. The stakes are high. He hardly hides his feelings of urgency, impatience, and, towards the opponents, biting irony. The section begins with a harsh address ("O foolish Galatians!" 3:1) and closes with a caustic attack ("As for those agitators, they had better go the whole way and make eunuchs of themselves!" 5:12, NEB). The difficult task modern interpreters have in deciphering the complexities of Paul's argument and the (to us) strained way he uses the Scripture should not lead to the conclusion that he is only engaged in detached theorizing. He is, in an exemplary way, the pastor-theologian.

The following outline gives a sense of the movement as well as the structure of the section.

1. 3:1–5   Appeal to the experience of the Galatian churches: How did you receive the Spirit?
2. 3:6–14   The blessing promised to Abraham has now come to the Gentiles.
3. 3:15–29   To belong to Christ is to be Abraham's heir and no longer to be under the suppression of the law.
   a. Vs. 15–18   The law does not invalidate the promise.
   b. Vs. 19–29   Christ's coming changes the status of the law and produces a new fellowship.
      i. Vs. 19–25   The law had a temporary function as custodian.
      ii. Vs. 26–28   Incorporation into Christ brings God's

children (Abraham's heirs) into a new
unity.
4. 4:1–11 Christ is decisive for freedom and adoption as God's children.
  a. Vs. 1–7 The situation of the heir changes with God's sending of his Son and his Spirit.
  b. Vs. 8–11 Beware of a lapse into slavery.
5. 4:12–20 Paul is perplexed about the plight of the Galatians.
6. 4:21–31 The law itself witnesses to the covenant of freedom.
7. 5:1–12 The Galatians are faced with the frightening implications of circumcision.

Galatians 3:1–5
Spiritual Beginnings

In numerous places throughout his letters Paul employs the categories of Jewish apocalyptic to serve as a matrix for an argument which has very much to do with present realities and not future speculation. For instance, at the beginning of chapter one the concept of the two ages provides the framework for affirming a decisive change which occurred in the experience of the Galatians whereby they were delivered from one era characterized by evil and set in another characterized by grace. To decide in favor of circumcision is to deny the nature of grace and to revert to the old age (1:3–9). Likewise, Paul warns the Galatians (4:8–10) that acceptance of the agitators' message puts them back under the slavery of the controlling powers of the old eon. At times this concept of the two ages is used by Paul to assert the radical character of life in Christ, so unlike anything previous (II Cor. 5:16–17); at other times it provides an opportunity to indicate the ephemeral nature of what may otherwise seem imposing or permanent (I Cor. 2:6; 7:29–31); at still other times it becomes the structure for designating the continuous warfare between good and evil (Eph. 6:12).

In verses 1–5 Paul uses the concept of the two ages to interpret the experience of the Galatian Christians in order to get them to face squarely the gravity of the issue before them.

65

It is as if they are in the hands of a magician who has cast a spell over them. They no longer see what at one time was so prominently displayed among them—the message of the crucified Christ. Thus Paul appeals to their beginnings as Christians, to their experience of entering the new age. How did they come to receive the Spirit, the supreme mark of the new age? By doing something, such as getting themselves circumcised, or by simply hearing the gospel which leads to faith? How do they account for the transforming experiences and the mighty works which occurred in their midst? Have they forgotten how it all happened and who made it happen? By harshly addressing the Galatians and by recalling their entrance into the new age Paul hopes to break the spell under which they currently seem to live.

The term "Spirit" is used for the first time in this letter in these verses and warrants an introductory, if only brief, comment. It reappears at decisive locations in the remaining chapters (3:14; 4:6, 29; 5:5; 6:8) and becomes a significant feature of Paul's description of the life of freedom (5:16–25). The Spirit is God's vital presence, his lively power operative in the church and in the world. Four aspects of the Spirit's appearance and activity emerge from the series of questions Paul poses for his readers in these verses.

1. The Spirit comes in and with the preaching of the crucified Christ. Something remarkable had happened to the Galatian Christians. They had been wrenched from the bondage, frustrations, and fears of the past and set in a brand new world. For some it may have been traumatic, for others puzzling; for still others it may have been like the completion of a long journey when one is safe and secure at home. God's Spirit had worked to bring about changes in the lives of individuals and to create a community of faith and support. He had become an energizing reality in their midst. But Paul's point in recalling the beginning of their new life is to remind them how it all came to be—through the preaching of the crucified Christ. There had been no talk of special rites or religious observances, no external validations of the Spirit's presence, nothing to be *done* to ensure God's favor. There had only been the public statement of the gospel which had led to faith and the reception of the Spirit.

66

These words of Paul are instructive, especially in a day when the search for meaning in life is often expressed in terms of a search for the Holy Spirit and the gifts connected with the Spirit. Individuals long for something more real than what can be found in a frantic, impersonal, and materialistic world. The very word "Spirit" becomes an attraction by suggesting an animating force, a reality giving ardor, vitality, and warmth of feeling. The quest, however sincere, nevertheless is open to distortion. For many reasons—perhaps the intensity of the search or the strangeness of "spiritual" language—God's freedom is often neglected in the pursuit of human freedom. In some cases, a particular ritual or a set of phrases become the ingredient essential in invoking the Spirit; in other cases, the absence of order or form is the key, an enforced spontaneity. What we learn from Paul's reflection of the experience of the Galatians, however, is that nothing—neither liturgical form nor the lack of it—assures the coming of the Spirit to a group or to individuals. God is free to act where and when he wills. But in the past he has accompanied the statement of the gospel with his Spirit. Seeking for the Spirit, then, means returning in faith to the message.

2. The Spirit is set in radical opposition to the flesh. Though Paul develops this contrast in more detail later (5:16–25), the introduction of it here (3:1–5) is interesting. "Having begun with the Spirit, are you now ending [i.e., trying to bring freedom to perfection] with the flesh?" Evidently part of the appeal of the agitators to the Gentile Christians in Galatia was the notion that circumcision with all it symbolized was like icing on the cake. It completed and even perfected the freedom of the gospel. Paul, however, declares such a move to be a fatal step backwards. The Spirit is that power which joins Christians to the new age; the flesh belongs to the enslaving but transitory world out of which they had been liberated. To forsake the new world would be sheer folly.

Paul's description of works of the law as "flesh" is intriguing. One expects to find the blatant sins he later lists as examples of the works of the flesh (5:19–21), but to categorize a religious rite like circumcision with things like immorality, impurity, licentiousness, and drunkenness is astounding. It points to a fact which the church in its history has continually rediscovered, namely that the more sinister enemies of the faith are not always the obviously irreligious practices of the world but often the potent forces of morality and religion which operate within. The latter tend to undermine the gospel by a preoccupation

67

with the particular form an obedient response ought to take. Rigid lines are drawn between those who do and those who do not, with the result that the law becomes again a dividing wall. The prodigal son is sent back into the far country, or at least banished from the family gatherings until he can get his act cleaned up. "God will show mercy if you simply do such-and-such." Unfortunately, the effort to avoid the Scylla of cheap grace often leads dangerously close to the Charybdis of works-righteousness.

3. The Spirit is the power of the new age and thus the source of vitality and mighty works. If more were known about the early days of the Christian communities in Galatia, we might more easily identify exactly what Paul has reference to in verses 4–5. Was the life of these congregations begun in the context of charismatic activity and extraordinary phenomena? Miracles are mentioned (3:5), and if the theory which argues that the epistle was directed to the churches of provincial Galatia (e.g., Antioch of Pisidia, Iconium, Lystra, Derbe) is correct, then the account of Paul's healing of the crippled man at Lystra found in Acts 14:8–10 might provide an example of one such miracle. Nothing is mentioned in Acts about speaking in tongues in these cities. In any case, Paul recalls for the Galatians a beginning in which the Spirit's activity had been prominent and productive. A small, but notable, change in the translation of the RSV makes this even more evident to the English reader. In the first edition verse 4 read, "Did you *suffer* so many things in vain?" connoting a time of persecution in their past. But later editions (and also the NEB, JB, TEV) reflect another meaning of the Greek verb, more positive and perhaps more suitable to the context: "Did you *experience* so many things in vain?"

Both the Hebrew and Greek words for "spirit" have also the meanings of "breath" and "wind," suggesting liveliness and power (cf. John 3:8). Often in the New Testament where the Spirit is present there are stupendous deeds and unusual activities, tokens of the breaking in of God's new age. But a caveat is in order. Such uncommon phenomena are not meant to be used as positive proof that God's Spirit is really at work. That is if remarkable things, such as healings, speaking in tongues, increased attendance, or enlarged budgets, are happening they do not in themselves represent unquestionable evidence that God is their source. In like manner if such noteworthy signs are absent, one cannot deduce that the Spirit is dormant or that

God has forsaken his people. The closest Paul comes to suggesting a test for ascertaining the presence of the Spirit is whether or not one is led to the basic confession, "Jesus is Lord" (I Cor. 12:3) and to the manifestation of his fruit: love, joy, peace, patience, kindness, goodness, faithfulness, gentleness, and self-control (5:22–23).

Alongside this warning, however, must be set Ernst Käsemann's words about the need for the liveliness of the Spirit.

> Christianity cannot entirely do without enthusiasm. That does not simply mean that the doctrine of the Holy Spirit is an essential part of theology and that without the reality of that Spirit revelation and church decay. It also means that a Christianity in which there are no signs and mighty works, no visible charismata, in which the "God is really among you" of 1 Cor. 14:25 is no longer heard from pagans in answer to its preaching, its actions, and its suffering, becomes empty, doctrinaire, and a form of ideology. ... No matter what danger enthusiasm may have brought to the church, the final defeat of enthusiasm has always signalized the sleeping church, even the busiest one. Enthusiasm is indispensable where the priesthood of all believers is to be awakened and the community represented and enlivened by the laity. There is no Christian freedom without a dose of enthusiasm (*Jesus Means Freedom,* pp. 51, 54).

4. The Spirit comes to the whole community and not simply to a few, select leaders. Paul gives no indication here that he is addressing an inner core of believers who in distinction from the entire congregation of Christians have received the Spirit. The Old Testament tells of sporadic manifestations of the Spirit in the lives of significant leaders and occasional groups within Israel, but the prophets looked beyond to the arrival of an era when God would give his Spirit to "all flesh" (cf. Joel 2:23–32; Acts 2:16–21). All would participate in the liveliness and strength of God's peculiar activity. This era is inaugurated with Christ's resurrection and the ensuing Pentecost, an era in which the Galatians had already come to share. It was "the promise of the Spirit" (3:14) fulfilled in their midst, enabling them to call God, "Abba, Father" (4:6). For Paul, belonging to Christ (i.e., to be a Christian) and receiving the Spirit are inseparable (cf. Rom. 8:9–17).

"Ordinary" Christians are from time to time overawed and even intimidated by the apparent spirituality of fellow-believers. They suppose that some have been more abundantly endowed by, or have a special aptitude for, the Spirit, setting them

69

apart from the rank and file of the church's membership. Paul's words are reassuring. He is opposed to any notion of a caste system within the church, any idea of cultivating elitist groups. To the Corinthian congregation which had in its midst a spiritual clique, he writes, "For by one Spirit we were all baptized into one body—Jews or Greeks, slaves or free—and all were made to drink of one Spirit" (I Cor. 12:13). Gifts will vary, personal experiences will differ, but all who respond in faith have already benefited from the Spirit's activity (though they may not express it in just that way) and are continually being addressed by that same Spirit when confronted by the comforts and demands of the gospel. The fact that the Spirit has worked in the whole community, and not in just a few, becomes later in the letter the basis for the ethical appeal Paul makes. To paraphrase, "Since the Spirit has given us life, let the Spirit direct the course of our life" (5:25).

The section which follows (3:6–14), though shifting from the Galatians' early experience to the consideration of Abraham, nevertheless continues the train of thought begun in verses 1–5. Paul's involved argument aims at the important conclusion that the promised Spirit, which has characterized the beginning of the Galatian congregations, is received by faith (3:14). This of course has been the primary point made in verses 1-5.

Galatians 3:6–14
Inheriting the Blessing of Abraham

The early church began as a sect of Judaism. Jesus was a Jew; the major figures in the initial growth of the church were Jews; the Old Testament was authoritative for both Christians and Jews. According to Acts, when Paul began his missionary outreach to non-Jews, his point of contact in visiting towns and cities was the synagogue. Exactly when the church "broke away" from Judaism in terms of being a distinctively different community without connecting links is difficult to date. Certainly Paul never outgrew his personal roots ("I myself am an Israelite . . ." Rom. 11:1) nor did he make any move that would suggest the church desired to be independent of Judaism. His

70

debates with the Jews were basically intramural. Christ had brought a radically new era in the history of God's relations with his people, but for Paul it was a newness very much in continuity with God's actions in Israel's past. Some scholars would argue that the most significant event in the separation of the church from the synagogue did not come until the last decade of the first century when a school of rabbis at Jamnia set out clear lines of demarcation which essentially excommunicated the Christians from Judaism.

The entrance of Gentiles into the Christian church forced a momentous issue, as the Epistle to the Galatians illustrates, precisely because people like Paul were not willing to ignore their Jewish roots and go their separate ways. Profoundly convinced that the gospel by its very character was intended for non-Jews as well as Jews, Paul was equally convinced that Jesus is the Messiah of Jewish expectation and the Christian faith a fulfillment of Scripture promises.

The theological problem posed by these convictions as well as by the circumstances in the church is the identification of who the people of God really are. Paul's solution has informed his discussion prior to this point in the letter, but in verses 6–29 he pointedly faces the issue. Since the Messiah has come as he has, that is, as a Jew and as the embodiment of God's free and limitless grace, who then makes up the people of God? What is the prime feature identifying such a people? Who are truly Abraham's descendants?

In the course of answering this fundamental question, Paul has to face another one which in part has been dealt with in chapter two: What is the place of the law, since the law (including circumcision) is the identifying feature of Judaism at this time?

The section 3:6–14 breaks neatly into three divisions. First, Paul introduces the figure of Abraham (3:6–9) and quotes two texts from Scripture associated with him (Gen. 15:6 and 12:3). With one he makes the point that God counted Abraham righteous in light of faith, and so Abraham's true descendants must be those who relate to God through faith. With the other he recalls God's promise which guaranteed that at some future time Gentiles would be blessed through Abraham's line, implying that the mission of the church outside the boundaries of Judaism is the fulfillment of an ancient promise.

In the second division (3:10–12) Paul cites a further passage

71

from the *torah* (Deut. 27:26) to show that those who rely on the law put themselves under the curse of that very law on which they depend. It is clear that the law simply cannot do for them what they desperately need. God's gift of life is received only through faith, as Hab. 2:4 states, the law being of a completely different order from faith. Finally, in the third division of the pericope (3:13–14) Paul describes how Christ removed the curse brought about by the law by becoming himself a curse in behalf of his people. An interchange occurs in which he represents the guilty and accepts their curse, while they in turn go free. The purpose of his action is to extend to the Gentiles the blessing promised to Abraham and to make possible the reception of the Spirit by faith.

The details of Paul's argument (3:6–14) are, frankly, difficult to follow. The texts from the Old Testament do not appear to say exactly what he concludes from them, and in the case of the citation from Habakkuk, Paul quotes a verse which differs significantly in meaning from both the Septuagint and the Masoretic texts. Still, the direction of Paul's thinking is clear. One must be careful in treating a passage like this not to miss the forest for the trees. It is easy to get bogged down in the details and never see the whole. For this reason, the double goal toward which Paul's argument moves in the section is important as a site to focus on: ". . . that in Christ Jesus the blessing of Abraham might come upon the Gentiles, that we might receive the promise of the Spirit through faith" (3:14). The verse ties his thinking in this passage to the primary thrust of the letter as a whole. Paul contends for the Gentiles among the people of God as those who in Christ have a rightful place with believing Jews as Abraham's heirs. In connection with this, Paul contends for the fact that the Spirit, the power of the new age, is experienced through faith.

Paul's logic in verses 6–14 goes like this: Since God reckoned his righteousness to Abraham by faith (so Gen. 15:6), then it is faith which distinguishes the true descendants of Abraham. His family is composed of persons who are set apart by belief, not by some other feature such as natural genealogy or the doing of works of the law. In fact, the law itself is evidence of this. It bears witness to the curse it places on people and from which Christ has freed them. Anyone who reads the law correctly knows who inherits the promises of God and how they are received. Abraham is not the father of circumcised Jews but

72

of all persons, Jews and Gentiles, who accept God's grace in faith.

But why Abraham? What is there in this character which led Paul to return to him often, and especially in a context like that of the letter to the Galatians? Several reasons are obvious. Abraham was the father of the Israelite people. If Paul can show that Gentiles are in Abraham's heritage, then they must be accepted in the church. The law came long after Abraham; therefore, promises made to him are not affected or conditioned in any way by what happened at Sinai. Circumcision became a special rite for Israel at the time of Abraham, and thus discussion about its continuing validity must take him into account. These factors may all have been in Paul's thinking when he reflected on the figure of Abraham.

There also may have been another reason. Abraham was not unknown to the rabbis of the first century. They also read Gen. 15:6 but interpreted Abraham's faith to be a work. His fidelity and upright integrity were rewarded by God in being reckoned as righteousness. What is more, his faithfulness became the main deposit in a treasury of merit which could only be drawn on by Jews and not by Gentile proselytes. Paul's exegesis of Gen. 15:6 is of course diametrically opposite to that of the rabbis. He interprets the reckoning of righteousness as an act of God's grace, not as a payment for Abraham's constancy (cf. Rom. 4:1–8). Furthermore, Gen. 12:3, a text whose universalist elements are generally omitted in the rabbinic treatments of Abraham, is set alongside Gen. 15:6, to clarify that God's act of grace is not limited to Abraham's physical descendants. It may well be that Paul's attention to Abraham is in part due to his desire to counter a false understanding of faith and works stirred in the Galatians by some version of the rabbinic interpretation.

Three of Paul's concerns come to expression in these verses.

1. God is faithful to his promise. Gal. 3:8 contains the citation of Gen. 12:3, probably the Old Testament quotation most crucial to Paul's argument in chapter three. "In you shall all the nations be blessed." Variously he refers to this word as "gospel" (3:8), "blessing" (3:9, 14), and "promise" (3:15ff). The movement of the Christian message to the Gentiles is not just Paul's pet project, a decision to widen the mission the way a business enlarges by setting up branch offices. It has been a part of God's

intention from the beginning, explicit in the call to Abraham.

Several interpreters have noted the distinction between a prediction and a promise. A prediction is a declaration in advance that a particular event will occur or a certain result will ensue. The one making the prediction may have little or no stake in the outcome. In fact, today in searching for the best prediction it is often wise to turn to one who knows well the situation but is personally unaffected. That individual is less likely to confuse the prediction with wishful thinking. A promise, on the other hand, is a pledge to do something specific. The promiser gives his or her word to make good, to keep faith with the pledge. Gen. 12:3 is a promise made to Abraham, and Paul is calling attention to the fact that God has kept his word. He is reliable. The opponents in Galatia would of course agree with that in principle, but the question is how will God's promise be fulfilled—on the basis of faith or some other connection with Abraham.

2. Paul uses citations from the "law" to condemn those who rely on the law. Of the six quotations from the Old Testament in verses 6–14, five are from the Pentateuch and one from the Prophets. By employing these references, Paul is in effect arguing here what he later makes explicit, "You who desire to be under law, do you not hear the law?" (4:21).

Paul uses the word "law" (the Greek *nomos*) in several different senses and at times mixes the meanings in a single context. It is virtually impossible to determine a specific meaning for each usage, but the vast majority falls into one of two categories: (a) the Mosaic law, that is, the Pentateuch, but without differentiation between legal and non-legal material; (b) the Old Testament as a whole. In addition, "law" may mean a specific commandment; the sense of demand, constraint, or necessity; a norm or principle; the Jewish religion, since its distinguishing feature is its possession of the law; or "the law of Christ." While it is essential to be aware of the variety of meanings "law" can have, it is equally important to remember that Paul uses a single word for these various meanings.

The point he makes in verses 6–14 is that the law, the Pentateuch, does not offer two ways of salvation—one based on human performance in keeping the commandments and another based on a divine activity to which humans respond by faith. The law from the beginning has indicated only one way of salvation, and that is something done by God and not by

74

humans. The person who *really* keeps the law realizes that the law can never justify and so puts his trust in the faithfulness of God. Paul's complaint with the agitators in Galatia is not that they devote too much attention to the law, but that they read it wrongly and distort its meaning. They take what he in another place calls "holy, just and good" (Rom. 7:12) and put it in the service of the demonic forces (4:8–10). They fail to hear that the law contains a promise of the gospel (3:8).

James A. Sanders has shed considerable light on the subject of Paul's use of the law by pointing to the Jewish tradition lying behind Paul. The Hebrew *torah,* which the Septuagint consistently translates as *nomos* (law), is the term for the divine revelation given at Sinai. It comes to be written down as the Pentateuch and thus is composed of an intermingling of narrative and legal code. The narrative or story dimension, called *haggadah,* serves to answer for Israel the question of identity, "Who are we?"; the legal dimension (both moral and ceremonial codes), called *halakah,* serves to answer the question of life-style, "What are we to do?" *Torah* is never exclusively one or the other, but a blend of the two. The fundamental difference, Sanders argues, between rabbinic Judaism and Pauline Christianity is the perspective on *torah.* Rabbinic Judaism read it predominantly in terms of *halakah,* as a code-book to provide laws for the living of life. Paul, on the other hand, stressed the *haggadic* aspect, calling attention to it as a story of God's works of righteousness in ancient Israel. He

> in facing his mandate . . . to preach the gospel to the Gentiles, found it well to emphasize Torah as the story of divine election and redemption, in the eschatological conviction that God's recent work in Christ had made that election and that redemption available to all mankind, while at the same time to de-emphasize those specific stipulations which seemed to present stumbling-blocks to carrying out the mandate and which seemed to detract from the Torah-Gospel story of God's righteous acts which had found their culmination, goal, and climax in God's eschatological act in Christ ("Torah and Paul," in J. Jervell, and W. A. Meeks, eds., *God's Christ and His People,* p. 138).

If the story is read as a story of God's activity in Israel, then it becomes much more possible to see Jesus as God's decisive and climactic act completing the story.

75

Paul may not have articulated the division between narrative and legal code quite so neatly as Sanders, but the schema serves a useful purpose. The opponents in Galatia were definitely not strict adherents of rabbinic Judaism, for they acknowledged Jesus as the Messiah. But they still tended to read the *torah* as a collection of legal demands, as *halakah.* Paul vigorously attacks what this means in terms of requirements laid on the Gentiles, in effect a new bondage. In doing so, he does not, however, call for the total abolition of the law in the church. The polemical context evokes from him extremely negative comments (e.g., 3:19–25), but at the same time he cites the law repeatedly as if it still retained tremendous authority. It continues to have its place, both as a condemnation of those who rely on it for their own justification and as a promise of the redemption coming in Christ. It relates the story which climaxes in Jesus' advent, death, and resurrection, with the result that those who respond in faith actually become part of the story as Abraham's heirs. When Paul highlights the role of Abraham and particularly the promise God made to him in Gen. 12:3, he is reminding his readers of the *haggadic* aspect of the law. The modern Christian will also find this a salutary reminder when reading the Old Testament, especially when confronted with the large amount of legal material.

In addition, Paul provides some clues for us in this passage about the nature of the conversation today between Jews and Christians. Usually when such groups gather in local settings for discussion, the primary topics are either those things which the two share in common or community problems which need the attention of both. Given the bleakness of past history, the nurture of trust and acceptance is essential. Assuming that the interest is more than sociological, however, there always comes the point when the discussion of differences needs to be risked if the relationship is ever going to progress. What better place to start than with the basic issue at stake when the two began to move apart? This issue for Paul is surely not the question of who is responsible for the death of Jesus, but of how one reads the *torah* and thus what meaning *torah* can continue to have in light of the coming of Jesus as Messiah.

3. Christ took on himself the curse of the law, liberating humanity from what it rightfully deserved and ushering in the new age. Paul turns to the work Christ accomplished in relation to the law (3:13–14). In doing so, he employs a sentence structure familiar from other texts (4:4–5; II Cor. 5:13–15, 21; I Thess. 5:9–10; cf. John 17:19; I Pet. 2:24), which may indicate that the

verses are a piece of a traditional formula. *Christ* does something *for us*, in order that *we might receive* (or *become*) something. The result is an interchange. Christ, the innocent, has become accursed for his people, so that his people, the accursed, might be exonerated. He shares fully in the human plight, even to the extent of a degrading death, thereby effecting the needed redemption. We shall return to this point in connection with chapter 4, verses 4–5.

But what is "the curse of the law"? On whom does it fall, and why? Verse 10 says that it falls on those who rely on their own fulfillment of the law's demands and on those who fail to keep the whole law (so the quote from Deut. 27:26). This, one way or another, includes the whole of Judaism. But Gentiles are not exempt either, because they are aliens to the law, strangers to the covenants of Israel, and without circumcision. The law by its exclusiveness "curses" Gentiles, unless they are prepared to become proselytes. The "us," therefore, whom Christ redeemed embraces both Jews and Gentiles.

It is a remarkable story of how a curse is turned into a blessing. The pride of those who trust their own accomplishments, the frustration and guilt of those who continue to fail despite their good intentions, the estrangement of the outsiders who have to sacrifice their identity if they want to be included —Christ assumes it all. In its place he gives a new fellowship transcending any and all division, full participation with him in God's community, and the constant endowment of the life and power of the new age. The threat of the law is over and gone. Death by crucifixion (though the quotation from Deut. 21:23 in context speaks of the impalement of bodies after execution) which connoted for Jews ignominy and scandal becomes the occasion whereby God's promises made long ago are fulfilled.

Galatians 3:15–29
The Role of the Law

Throughout the larger section, Gal. 3:6–29, Paul is concerned with the question as to who is the true Israel. In verses 6–14, as we have seen, he begins with Abraham and argues that Abraham's descendants are those who, like Abraham, respond to the faithfulness of God. In the light of the promise given in Gen. 12:3 and fulfilled in Christ, it is obvious that national and ethnic considerations no longer count; the door is now open to the world. Christ is the one who has caused the redefinition of the people of God, because he has taken on himself the curse of the law and has made possible the giving of Abraham's blessing to non-Jews.

In making this argument for a new understanding of the people of God, Paul is aware of one big issue he must confront: What about the law? The *torah* has been Israel's pride and joy; the psalmists of old sang its glories (Ps. 1:2; 19:7–11; 119). Particularly since the reestablishment of religious life by Ezra after the exile, the *torah* has been Judaism's distinguishing symbol. It was read in synagogues not only in Palestine but throughout the dispersion. Though the temple was sacked and the land snatched away, Jewish existence could continue because the *torah* was present. It made Israel to be Israel. If Paul is then to present different criteria for determining who constitutes the people of God, he cannot avoid discussing what place the law will occupy in the redefinition. This he seeks to do in verses 15–29.

In the first paragraph of the section (3:15–18) Paul clarifies the relation between the promise and the law by pointing out that the former preceded the latter by four hundred and thirty years. Since the promise (in terms of the covenant or will) is made and confirmed by God, there is no way the law coming later can abrogate or modify it. Here and in verse 19 where he mentions the origin of the law, Paul may be correcting a notion prevalent in rabbinic Judaism which attributed to the *torah* a preexistent status. It was older than the world and had a part in the act of creation. In one sense, God himself was bound to the law in that he had studied it and fulfilled it. Paul, however, now approaches the law in terms of the promise made to Abraham and fulfilled in Christ. For him the law takes its place in the historical scheme with Moses, to whom it was given.

In verses 19–25 he moves a step further by saying why God provided the law—"because of transgressions." Sin of course had been in the world since Adam, but for Paul it was viewed in a different light before Moses. The advent of the law turned unconscious wrong-doing into known, willful, disobedience, to the end that something could be done about it (cf. Rom. 5:12–14; 7:7). The law defined deeds and the lack of deeds in

78

terms of God's purposes. It named the demons, or as the somewhat interpretive translation of verse 19 in the NEB reads, it
made "wrong-doing a legal offence." As such, it consigned all
human acts to sin, at least for a definite period of time. Its role
was a custodial one, with power to detain and even enslave
(4:3), but not to liberate. Rather than aligning itself against the
promise, the law served a specific function, albeit in a negative
way, by closing down all avenues of escape, until Christ should
come.

Most commentators are quick to point out—and for good
reason—that in verse 24 the word *paidagogos* should be
translated as "custodian" (RSV) or "tutor" (NEB) rather than
"school-master" (KJV). In wealthy Greek and Roman families
the *paidagogos* was the individual, usually a slave, entrusted
with the care of the child at those times when the child was not
at school. The translation "school-master" has often led to the
notion that the law has a continuing function as educator, and
in this context of course that is a negative function. It humiliates
sinners by exposing their folly and failures, or it crushes their
self-righteousness and pride leaving them guilty and totally
without hope. They must encounter first the law with its inexo-
rable demand creating anxiety and doubt before they are in a
position to receive the healing and forgiving grace of the gospel. This interpretation is not entirely false. Outside of Christ
the law can only identify wrong and condemn it. But Paul
speaks historically, not existentially (3:22–25). He is not thinking
of the way sinners come to Christ, via the law, but of the role
the law played until the coming of the Messiah, who by fulfilling
the law and taking its curse made its custodial function obsolete.
"But now that faith [meaning Christ and the availability of faith
in him] has come, we are no longer under a custodian" (3:25).

But Paul is not writing merely as a historian who divides
the biblical time-line into three periods: from Adam to Moses
(before the law); from Moses to Christ (the law functioning as
custodian); from Christ on (the law no longer a custodian).
There is also an inner connection between the law and Christ,
perhaps obscured somewhat in the RSV. Verse 25 which reads,
"So that the law was our custodian *until Christ came*" could just
as accurately read "*. . . with a view to Christ's coming.*" Probably both temporal and purposive ideas are to be understood.
The law as a custodian served an essential function leading up
to as well as ending with the advent of Christ.

79

Paul is certainly in a position to speak about the law. In his pre-Damascus Road days his attitude was that of an orthodox Pharisee. He delighted in the law and zealously kept its precepts. His comment about being "blameless" (Phil. 3:6) need not imply that he imagined he was without fault, but that in times of failure he had availed himself of the law's own means of restitution and pardon. It was his passion, and thus he set about persecuting any who claimed a relationship to God outside its boundaries. But the appearance of Christ to Paul changed all that. To think of salvation in terms of the law now would be to revert to a pre-Christian time. True freedom is found in the promise, not the law. It is an inclusive promise, which in the light of Christ's coming results in an amazing unity of Jew and Greek, slave and free, male and female.

Careful readers of the Bible today can appreciate Paul's need to deal as forcefully as he does with the issue of the law because of the context out of which he came and for which he was writing. Still, the inevitable question arises: What part should the Mosaic law play in the life and theology of the church? Paul is very negative, leading some to conclude that the law has no place at all in the church (3:15–29). Yet in another place he describes the law as "holy, just, and good," something to delight in (Rom. 7:12, 23). If God's salvation comes through his grace alone and human performance is in no way a precondition to grace, then what use is the law? Are not all of the ritual rules and the moral demands outdated?

Paul of course is not writing for the twentieth century church and does not answer directly all the questions one might want to put to him. Too often he has been disengaged from his context and dragged into the modern era to support this or that theory in a proof-text fashion. On the other hand, one of the tasks of the theologian is to listen to a biblical writer like Paul and on the basis of what he says to take the risk of dealing with contemporary questions. What, therefore, in the light of 15–29 and some other passages in the letter, can be said about the place of the Mosaic law in the church?

Negatively, two brief comments need to be made. First, the law can no longer be a wedge to divide people. For first century Judaism the split came not so much between Jews who were morally superior because they kept the law and other Jews who were less zealous or even indifferent to it completely. The law was a prerogative given to all Jews; it was a national as well as a religious symbol. The coming of Christ, however, involves a redefinition of the people of God. The new unity discovered in fellowship with him replaces the old lines of demarcation which included some and excluded others. As previously noted, Paul returns time and again to this theme in Galatians as he contends for the rightful place of the Gentiles in the church. Secondly, the law can no longer be a threat. Its curse is gone; its custodial role is at an end. To be terrorized now by its stringent demands and to feel the anxiety of its condemnation is to forget that Christ has taken its curse. There may be places in the church where proof-texts from the law are still hurled in anger and judgment at those whose conduct is less than perfect, but that, too, is to live anachronistically as if Christ had never come.

The situation, however, in most circles today is not that the law either divides or threatens people; it is more often ignored. Its stories and commands are written off as belonging to a bygone era, primarily nomadic or agrarian, where polygamy prevailed and life was cheap. What *positive* value does the law have? In the third chapter of Galatians Paul has undeniably devalued the law in relation to the exalted place it occupied in Judaism, but even in this polemical context he never suggests that the words of the law should be forgotten. It is from confinement *under* law that Christ redeems his people.

(a) The law is thus important to the church because it witnesses to the salvation which comes in Christ. By "law" Paul means in this chapter not an abstract imperative or a universal sense of oughtness but the Mosaic law, given at Sinai and in its written form embracing narrative as well as legal material. He can even use the term synonymously with "scripture" (3:22; cf. 3:8). In verses 6–14 he can quote from it to document the point that God had intended the blessing of Abraham to include the Gentiles. In verses 21–25, where admittedly the definition of law narrows and the emphasis falls more on its demand than its story, he acknowledges that it renders a service in preparation for Christ's coming by closing all other exits to the confinement. To change the metaphor, the law functions, like blinders on a horse, to point Israel in one direction—to the advent of the new age and the fulfillment of the promise.

The church still needs this witness because without it the New Testament makes little sense. Christ is the climax of a story which includes Sinai, with the giving of the Decalogue and the

81

establishment of the cult. To neglect the story is to rob Christ of his particular roots, one who was "born of a woman, born under the law" (4:4). The law identifies what sort of God it is who sends his Son and adopts others as his children. It defines for the church exactly what this family is like, where it came from, and what it is called to be. Undoubtedly the dawn of the new age brings a discontinuity with the past, with the result that God's people find their identity now in Christ and not in the law. But the discontinuity must be kept in proper balance with the continuity, which lays the foundation, provides the context, and gives meaning to the Christian gospel.

(b) This leads to a second reason why the church needs the Mosaic law, a reason Paul appropriately does not mention until later (5:14 and 6:2).

> For the whole law is fulfilled in one word, "You shall love your neighbor as yourself."
>
> Bear one another's burdens, and so fulfill the law of Christ.

The law is instructive for the Christian community as it lives out its life in the world. Christians are no longer "under the law" (5:18) but nevertheless can be guided by the law in facing all sorts of moral and ethical dilemmas. It is very significant that after all the denigration of the law in verses 19–25 Paul should still use the word in describing responsible freedom. It is of course the law now fulfilled in Christ. To return to James A. Sanders' comment cited in the previous section, *torah* (*nomos*, law) is composed of both narrative and legal code, never exclusively the one or the other. Paul in reading the *torah* as a narrative has come to see Jesus as the decisive chapter in an otherwise unfinished story. He is the one to whom the *torah* is directed. But that does not mean a negation of the legislative dimension of the *torah*, only a fresh perspective on it. He can call it "the law of Christ" (cf. I Cor. 9:20–21). By that he does not mean a different code or document; it is still the Mosaic law, but summed up in the command to love and interpreted in the light of Christ.

More will be said about this later (in connection with 5:13–15), particularly the way love radicalizes the law. It deepens demands and makes them more thorough-going and pervasive. At the same time, the command to love does not replace the law, as if the law having been summarized were no longer necessary. Love does not always tell one exactly how to respond

82

or what to say in the many ambiguous situations people face daily. Neither does the law; but in numerous cases passages like the ten commandments when read in the light of Christ give positive definition to the loving will of God. They help to prevent love from becoming soft sentimentality or merely an abstract principle. The church still needs the law to throw light on the human situation and love to keep that law from being rigidly interpreted.

Galatians 3:26–29
Unity and Equality

In many respects the section to which we now turn serves as the climax of the entire epistle. From the very beginning Paul has championed the cause of unity in Christ. The reason he went to Jerusalem a second time to see James, Peter, and John was to assure the fact that his mission among the Gentiles was not splitting the early community into Jewish and non-Jewish branches. Mutual recognition was an important implication of the faith he was called to preach. When Paul had to confront Peter at Antioch, it was over a question of church unity and how that unity reflected the integrity of the gospel. Throughout chapter three, Paul redefines the people of God so as to demonstrate that Jews and Gentiles belong together as a community constituted on the basis of God's faithfulness to his promise. The redefinition is now given a more positive turn and with a revolutionary explicitness that has had profound repercussions in the life of the church to this day.

". . . for in Christ Jesus you are all sons of God, through faith." Though the RSV (unlike all other recent translations) loses some of the strength of verse 26 by failing to begin a new sentence, the immediacy and force are still striking. Paul has reached a high point in his argument with the Galatians and addresses them directly. The shift is clean and sharp—from "we" to "you," from slavery under a custodian to life as heirs, from the law to Christ, from division and exclusiveness to the emphatic "all." The predominant motif is the change of control which has occurred so that no longer do the people of God look to the law as their distinguishing mark, their symbol of identity,

83

but to Christ. As if he wants to make sure that no one misunderstands him, Paul says it repeatedly: "in Christ Jesus" (3:26), "baptized into Christ" (3:27), "have put on Christ" (3:27), "one in Christ Jesus" (3:28), "Christ's," that is, belong to Christ (3:29). Being incorporated into Christ qualifies persons as Abraham's descendants. Since Christ is *the* seed of Abraham (3:16), it is identification with him rather than with the law that assures inclusion in the promise.

In emphasizing a change of control and in pointing to a new means of identification for Israel, is Paul talking about something which occurred in approximately A.D. 30 or something which happens in the experiences of persons when they respond in faith? On the one hand, as indicated in the previous section, Paul is speaking historically. Clauses like "till the offspring should come" (3:19) and "until Christ came" (3:24) can hardly be interpreted as meaning the existential moment in the lives of individuals when they become cognizant of the reality of Christ. Thus similar expressions using the word "faith" ("until faith should be revealed," 3:23; and "now that faith has come," 3:24) imply also the death and resurrection of Christ and the availability of faith in *him.* On the other hand, Paul speaks of baptism into Christ (3:27), surely intending by that the sacramental rite in which individuals participate as they publicly enter the church.

Since evidence can be cited for either option, it would seem that the answer to the question should be, both. Paul is pointing to Jesus *and* to the experience of individual Christians. He is equally interested in Christ and in the personal encounter with him by believers. But to put the answer this way is inadequate. Paul's overwhelming stress falls on the momentous happening at the beginning of the Christian era when God acted decisively for the whole human race. Something took place unlike any other historical occurrence. To speak in technical terms, Christ's coming was an eschatological event. It was world-changing; it inaugurated the last times. Though not every individual has been aware of that event and its implications, the event is nevertheless true and impinges on the lives of all. Christ's lordship is not a potentiality which is actualized when individuals are baptized; it is a reality which people either obey or disobey (by following some other lord). Baptism, then, is the occasion when the believer by God's grace is drawn into that lordship with other believers and so "puts on Christ." It is a time for celebrating what God's grace has done for the individual, not for celebrating that Jesus has finally become Lord. The stress Paul puts on the once-and-for-allness of the coming of Christ has helped to remind the church that it is not a mystery cult (like so many ancient religions) nor is its faith purely mysticism. It is rooted in an event in history which changed the course of that history.

Paul further describes the reality of Christ's dominion by saying, "There is neither Jew nor Greek, there is neither slave nor free, there is neither male nor female; for you are all one in Christ Jesus" (3:28). Perhaps behind such a radical statement is that Judeo-Christian conviction that God is one and that, since he is one, he must be the God of the Gentiles as well as the Jews (so also of slaves and free, of males and females). Paul argues this way in Rom. 3:29–30, and very effectively too, since the premise of the logic is fundamental to Israel's faith (cf. Deut. 6:4–5). But more explicit here is a christological rather than a theological conviction. "You are all one in Christ Jesus." Christ's death as a means of salvation excludes all other means; he creates one community, not many; thus there can no longer be barriers separating otherwise disparate groups. Circumcision implied division between Jew and non-Jew and between male and female. Baptism into Christ means unity.

But what sort of unity does Paul contemplate? What happens to the ethnic, social, and sexual distinctions between people? The three sets of polarities Paul mentions are not exactly parallel. One is born either male or female, and that is that (at least for Paul's day). One is born a Jew or not a Jew, though the categories are not so ultimately determined as the male-female differentiation. On the other hand, there is nothing inherent in the makeup of either slaves or non-slaves which unalterably fixes their fates. Changes in status were not at all uncommon. Free people, usually for economic reasons, could find themselves in slavery, while the manumission of slaves, unlike the practice of a more recent era, was a regular occurrence. Though the three sets of polarities are not parallel, Paul makes no distinction between them. If Paul himself is taken as a model, one must say that the differences between the categories remain. He continues to reflect a Jewish self-consciousness (cf. Gal. 2:15; II Cor. 11:22; Phil. 3:5; Rom. 11:14), to treat Jews and Gentiles as ethnic units (cf. Rom. 9–11), to address slaves, slave-owners, men and women as distinct groups. In the light of this,

85

the unity he declares is not one, in the first instance, in which ethnic, social, and sexual differences vanish, but one in which the barriers, the hostility, the chauvinism, and the sense of superiority and inferiority between respective categories are destroyed. Being in Christ does not do away with Jew or Greek, male or female, even slave or free, but it makes these differences before God irrelevant.

At the same time, the new unity given in Christ has tremendous social implications. The very fact that the differences no longer matter means that Christians must treat people and groups in this light not only in church on Sunday but in the total affairs of life, in the so-called secular arena as well as the sacred. Paul certainly makes a solid beginning at this. In 2:11–14 he defends the right of Gentiles to be present with Jews on a common basis at a social gathering. It is not just at worship services that the Jew-Gentile distinction is rendered irrelevant.

As for the slavery question, Paul sets a direction in his handling of Onesimus, the runaway slave. He returns him to his owner Philemon "no longer as a slave but more than a slave, as a beloved brother . . . *both in the flesh* and in the Lord" (Phile. 16). The reason Paul gives for sending him back at all is to demonstrate Philemon's goodness (Phile. 13–14). It is true that in I Cor. 7:20–22 Paul seems to suggest that slaves should merely accept their plight and not work to be freed, but the verses are ambiguous and come in a context where he also discourages the Corinthians from marrying unless necessary. He anticipates that the end will come soon. "I think that *in view of the impending distress* it is well for a person to remain as he is" (I Cor. 7:26). The "household rules" found in Ephesians and Colossians probably originated in the common life of the early church and not with Paul, but they, too, are interesting. Slaves are exhorted to be obedient to their masters, while the status of master is totally relativized by the reminder that masters also have a Master (the Greek is *kurios,* Lord) in heaven, with whom there is no partiality (Eph. 6:9; Col. 4:1).

One is left with the conclusion that though Paul never attacks slavery head-on as an institution, in Gal. 3:28 (cf. Col. 3:11) and in his dealings with Onesimus he does leave some pointed clues as to what the stance of the church ought to be. Unfortunately the later history of the church is not universally commendable. At times individuals discovered Paul's revolutionary insights and engaged heroically in the struggle to abolish slavery. At too many other times, however, the church claimed it had only a spiritual responsibility to slaves and either defended the owners or washed its hands of the whole issue. In any case, it was a later period which saw the implications of Paul's gospel worked out in most areas of the world (though in some places the struggle is still going on).

The story in regard to equality of the sexes is analogous to that of abolition. Paul's statements about women are also revolutionary if a bit ambiguous. There is Gal. 3:28 and there are other passages where he affirms a healthy interdependence between male and female (cf. I Cor. 11:11–12), statements extremely radical for a former Pharisee. He mentions women by name from time to time and always on a par with men, never in a condescending or patronizing fashion (cf. Rom. 16; Phil. 4:2–3). One gets the clear impression that he happily worked side by side with a number of women in his various missionary travels and saw them as partners and not subordinates. In I Cor. 14:34–35 women are enjoined from addressing the congregation, but this passage is likely a later interpolation. It disrupts the flow of the argument and contradicts I Cor. 11:2–16 where mention is made of women participating with men in praying and prophesying. The "household rules" of Ephesians and Colossians describe the submissive role wives play in relation to their husbands (Eph. 5:22–23; Col. 3:18–19), but the Pauline authorship of these letters is in doubt. At the same time, Paul does not openly and vigorously attack the oppression of women anymore than he attacks the institution of slavery.

If the parallel with slavery is correct (and it seems inescapable), then the task of the church is to listen to Paul's revolutionary insights, to shed its dominant male orientation (for the sake of men as well as women), and to discover the fellowship which can occur only when all members are truly free. In some places that struggle is well on its way, not without conflict and pain; in other places it has yet to begin. To say that the church should only be interested in the spiritual development of women and men and should avoid all discussion of the social import of equality in Christ is like saying the church should never have involved itself in fighting the institution of slavery. The fact is that Gal. 3:28 has enormous implications which Paul himself could hardly grasp, much less implement, and which remain for the church to carry out.

Yet Paul's witness is not the only one in the New Testament. There are other passages, in addition to the "household rules" mentioned above, which seem to advocate a submissive

87

role for women (e.g., I Tim. 2:8–15; I Pet. 3:1–6). On what basis does one choose Gal. 3:28 as *the* text to illumine the others? Why not use the so-called subordinationist texts to interpret Gal. 3:28?

Two comments are necessary by way of an answer. First, each text (including Gal. 3:28) must be read in terms of its historical context. Biblical texts initially communicated God's message to ancient readers and hearers, and only after having "overheard" that message can one consider their relevance for the contemporary community. Given the cultural and social circumstances of the Graeco-Roman world of the first century, many passages in the New Testament which convey a conservative message to modern readers were in fact revolutionary words in their original contexts. Eph. 5:21—6:9 is such a passage, with its direct and sobering injunctions to husbands and slave-owners. To ignore the specific character and direction of the passage and turn it into "timeless truth" is to miss its historical meaning. Thus one is always wary of any attempt to lift texts from their initial settings and string them together with other texts to produce *the* biblical view of this or that issue.

Second, there are, moreover, instances in the Bible where writers have shared the perspective of the prevailing culture on a particular matter. In such cases, Paul K. Jewett has suggested a return to an ancient principle of exegesis called "the analogy of faith." The principle says simply that the meaning of a text must correspond to the clear teaching of Scripture as a whole, to "the faith" rooted in the Bible. Jesus in a sense employed this method himself. When queried about divorce by the Pharisees, he did not deny that the Mosaic law allowed for divorce. He rather went back to the creation narratives (Gen. 1:27; 2:24; cf. 5:2) to find a word about the true intention of marriage and on the basis of this criticized Moses' commandment as an accommodation to Israel's hardness of heart. The provision for divorce was not analogous to "the faith" (Mark 10:2–9). In like manner, the equality between female and male in Christ corresponds to the fundamental message of the Bible about the relation of the sexes, and in light of this correspondence the passages about an inferior role for women must be interpreted as accommodations to the cultural patterns of the first century. Jewett sums up the case:

> To put matters theologically, or perhaps we should say hermeneutically, the problem with the concept of female subordina-

tion is that it *breaks the analogy of faith.* The basic creation narratives imply the equality of male and female as a human fellowship reflecting the fellowship of the Godhead; and Jesus, as the perfect man who is truly in the image of God, taught such equality in his fellowship with women so that one may say—must say—that "in Christ there is no male and female." Any view which subordinates the woman to the man is not analogous to but incongruous with this fundamental teaching of both the Old and New Testaments. To affirm that woman, by definition, is subordinate to man, does not correspond to the fundamental radicals of revelation; rather it breaks the analogy of faith (*Man as Male and Female*, p. 134).

The redefinition of the people of God is now complete. Before the coming of Christ that people's pride was the law; it was the gift of God which set her apart as a special people, unlike other nations and religions. By attention to the law she sought to maintain her privileged position as the chosen of God. Then the Messiah came, and the question of who really belongs to God's people was transformed. Christ fulfilled a promise to Abraham which had to do with the expansion of his family to include non-Jews, that is, those who do not have the Mosaic law as a component in their heritage. The people of God no longer is determined by the law but by Christ, belonging to him, being joined to him in baptism. But to redefine God's people in this way is to imply revolutionary consequences for the nature of the new fellowship.

The next stage in Paul's argument (4:1–11) is a further elaboration of the motifs of chapter three—the movement from being minors with no rights to becoming full-fledged children with free access to the Father—with a warning of the disastrous effects of retreating to a pre-Christian status.

Galatians 4:1–11
Freedom and Adoption

In responding to the argument of his opponents in Galatia, Paul writes with a vivid pen, employing images with telling force. His language, even when dealing with the complex issues of the nature of Israel and the function of the law, is graphic and lively. The sense of urgency prevents his ever settling down to an unimaginative or plodding style. At times it is difficult to know how far to push his picture-words. Precisely because they are so expressive, differences in interpretation arise when one commentator stresses a particular nuance which another commentator neglects. Occasionally the figures of speech overlap, posing the question as to whether or not the overlapping may be deliberate. Readers may complain, with justice, that Paul's prose is not always transparently clear, but they can hardly accuse him of dull pedantry.

In chapter three he made use of two striking images in describing the law and its place prior to the coming of Christ. The law was a jailor, who locked up the prisoners and kept guard over their confinement. No escape was possible until Christ came to liberate them (3:22–23). Then, the law also served as a custodian, one who took care of the children, directed all their activities, and tended to their discipline. Both expressions are evocative and suggestive. The negative task of the law might have been discussed with more precision in a lengthy treatise but hardly with more vigor. In chapter four Paul employs a third image, again with unusual effectiveness. Before Christ's coming the plight of people is compared to that of an heir, whose father has died and has set in his will a time when the child can have access to the family estate. Until he comes of age, the minor has no rights at all; his status is no better than that of a slave. He is under the control of guardians and trustees who manage his affairs and determine his life. The analogy, despite the mixing of the language of being an heir with adoption as children, is forceful. In light of the two previous images in chapter three, Paul does not even have to say that the guardians and trustees represent the law; that is clear. Further, the analogy becomes a serviceable device to affirm the decisive importance of Christ's appearance. "When the time had fully come [i.e., the time set by the father], God sent forth his Son . . ." (4:4).

In examining the passage, we shall follow three steps. First, it is necessary briefly to take note of the structure of verses 1–11 and observe the movement of thought throughout. Then, three specific exegetical problems need consideration since what one decides about them affects the resulting interpretation. Thirdly, we shall explore several affirmations made in the passage, which have had and continue to have theological importance.

90

1. The passage is composed of two distinct, yet closely related, paragraphs. The first begins with the analogy (4:1–2) and draws an immediate connection. As the minor is under the

control of the guardians and trustees, so "we" were minors in subjection to the elemental spirits of the world (4:3). Then, Paul identifies two connected steps in God's activity towards the world aimed at changing the situation of the minor. In one, he sends his Son, who thoroughly enters into the human situation as a minor and who by doing so effects the release of the minors and, mixing the metaphor, brings about their adoption as God's children (4:4–5). In the other, God sends the Spirit of his Son, who confirms in the experience of the adopted children that they really are a part of the family and can address God as "Abba, Father" (4:6). Verse 7 draws the first paragraph to a close by personalizing the result of God's activity (the "you" is second person *singular*). "So through God you are no longer a slave but a son, and if a son then an heir."

In the second paragraph, Paul again reflects on the situation of his readers before they became Christians (4:8) and warns them about returning to the slavery of their former days (4:9). By preoccupation with cultic affairs (4:10) they are simply putting themselves back under the demonic forces which are feeble and impotent, which can demand but never give. Paul even wonders whether he has not already lost the battle over his readers (4:11). The two paragraphs of the passage are bound together by the repetition of the word translated as "elemental spirits" (4:3,9). God has, by sending his Son and his Spirit freed people from bondage to these spirits. How can they possibly lapse into the same slavery again? The paragraph which follows (4:12–20) continues the personal probing Paul has begun with his readers (4:8–11), but this time in terms of his earlier relationship with them.

2. Three exegetical problems in the passage are perplexing. First, what can be said about the tremendous variation in the use of pronouns? Paul uses the first person plural, *we* and *our* (3:23–25); he shifts to the second person plural, *you* (3:26–29); he returns to the first person, *we* and *us* (4:3–5); both the second and first person are used, *you* and *our* (4:6); he uses the second person singular (4:7); and then he comes back to the second person plural (4:8–11). Some commentators argue that Paul throughout is drawing careful distinctions between Jewish Christians ("we") and Gentile Christians ("you") in calling attention to differing pasts out of which each comes—the Jews from slavery to the law, the Gentiles from slavery to pagan forces. This is the way Paul normally uses pronouns, that is, he

91

includes himself among Jewish Christians (cf. 2:15–17). The problem with this solution, however, is two-fold. First, it is impossible to draw a neat distinction consistently throughout the passage. For example, "we" (Jewish Christians) were slaves to the elemental spirits (4:3), but so were "you" (Gentile Christians) since "you" are tempted to turn back *again* to bondage (4:9). The pasts of both groups is interpreted as involving control by the elemental spirits. Further, the adopted children include both "we" (4:5*b*) and "you" (4:6*a*). Consequently, one can hardly argue that a careful discrimination is made throughout. Secondly, if a sharp distinction is intended between Jewish and Gentile Christians, how is one to explain verse 6, where both first and second person pronouns are used? Admittedly, the verse contains a difficult problem, as noted by the scribes who copied the Greek manuscripts prior to the days of printing. They made various changes in the text in order to cope with the awkwardness of "you" and "our" in the same sentence. A better solution to the problem of the varying pronouns is to say that Paul shifts about because one or the other group (Jewish or Gentile Christians) is more prominent in his mind but never exclusively so. He intends to convey that both were enslaved, the one group under the law, the other under the elemental spirits, prior to Christ's coming; both were freed by the sending of Christ and his Spirit; both are now children in one family; and both are vulnerable to a return to their previous condition. At various stages the argument may be more applicable to Jewish Christians than Gentile Christians, or *vice versa*, but never to the omission of the other. The same phenomenon of shifting from one personal pronoun to the other occurs in following verses also (4:26—5:1).

A second exegetical problem involves the phrase in verses 3 and 9 translated by the RSV as "the elemental spirits of the universe" (so also the NEB and TEV). Some translators prefer "the basic principles of the world" (so the NIV and JB). The former is based on the widespread belief in the Hellenistic world that human destiny was controlled by nonhuman forces, sometimes good, sometimes evil. Individuals were at the mercy of these powers of the unseen world and thus had little or no freedom to effect the course of their own lives. The latter translation assumes that the Greek word describes the rudimentary teachings, the ABC's of religion and the world. Linguistic data can be gathered to support either translation. Here the decisive

92

evidence comes in verse 8, where slavery is specified as bondage to "beings that by nature are no gods." When Paul speaks of reverting to this sort of slavery, he then must have in mind demonic forces or elemental spirits rather than basic or rudimentary principles.

The arresting feature of the phrase, however, is not its translation but the fact that Paul equates life under the law with bondage "to the elemental spirits of the universe." One can understand such a description for Gentiles who come from a pagan environment with its astrology and superstition, but Paul puts the entire non-Christian world in the same category. He is depicting the predicament of any person who is not set free by Christ. The Gentile Christians who are succumbing to the enticement of a secure place among the people of God (if they are circumcised and evidently keep the cultic calendar) are simply forfeiting their freedom and reverting to the old system of trying to propitiate the elemental spirits. They are rejecting the unity based on the gospel of grace and are opting for the past, where the forces they once served and will serve again are impotent. They are rather like ex-convicts who cannot stand the world of freedom and go back to prison to find security; like heirs who having come to the appointed time to enjoy the benefits of the family estate still long for their childhood and the control of guardians and trustees.

The third exegetical problem arises because two sets of images are mingled in a single paragraph. They tend to create confusion unless they are carefully distinguished. In the first three verses of chapter 4 Paul uses the analogy of the minor who awaits the time of adulthood when he can possess the family inheritance. The words "child" and "children" (4:1,3) refer to the subordinate position of those who have not yet come of age and can easily be translated as "minor" and "minors." However, Paul shifts to the language of adoption (4:5–6), and the term *sons* then refers to the homeless who have been brought into the family as full members. In the terms of the former analogy, Christ changes minors (who are no different from slaves) into adults; in the latter, he changes orphans into legally adopted children. Verse 7 mixes the two—"You are no longer a slave (as in 4:1) but a son (as in 4:5–6), and if a son then an heir (as in 3:29)."

3. Looking at the passage as a whole, one can observe several motifs of theological significance.

93

(a) God is the prime figure. He determines the appropriate moment for the new age to break into the old. He sends first his Son and then the Spirit of his Son. For the Gentiles who move from slavery to freedom, it is not so much a matter of coming to know God as it is coming to be known by God (4:9). Since the verb "know" here as in many other places connotes action, Paul is pointing to the experience which occurs when the Gentile Christians have been grasped by God, when the divine attention has been focused on them. This emphasis results in an unusual expression, "So *through God* you are no longer a slave but a son" (4:7). The more familiar phrase for Paul would be "through Christ." Again, the scribes in copying manuscripts amended the text in various ways to make the assertion less strange. Paul, however, wants to stress God's initiative and performance. Unlike the deities worshiped in the ancient world, God is involved in history and in the lives of people.

The contrast is especially striking here between God and the elemental spirits of the universe. Whereas the latter are feeble, helpless, like beggars who can only come with their hands out, God acts in a powerful way. He functions in his Son to set free those captive to the law and to take orphans into his family. The human condition, desperate as it may be, is not helpless before him. He does not wait on humanity to instigate a reclamation project for itself and then rush to support it. He does the reclaiming himself and, if that were not enough, sends his Spirit to incite in people an awareness of what he has done. One can think of numerous modern counterparts to the elemental spirits, which threaten always to enslave us, and whose track record reflects the same impotence in effecting true freedom. Beside God, the Father of Jesus Christ, they pale into insignificance.

(b) God's Son is sent forth "born of woman, born under the law." Verse 4 asserts the incarnation in a pointed and radical way. Jesus was wholly human with all the consequences relating to that. Not only was he flesh and bone as we are, he lived his life in complete solidarity with those "under the law." To use a distinction made by several theologians, he assumed the existence of Adam *after* the fall (cf. Rom. 8:3). He was vulnerable to all the conditions of human life which constantly threaten and unsettle—fear, loneliness, suffering, temptation, doubt, and ultimately godforsakenness. Though he did not sin—a fact the New Testament writers mention repeatedly (II Cor. 5:21; Heb.

94

4:15; I Pet. 2:22; I John 3:5)—he belonged to this transitory, sinful world and was subject to death.

Though the preexistence and incarnation of Christ are stated in verse 4, it is almost as if they are assumed in order to get at the critical issue, the liberation of those bound under the law. That is to say, there is nothing in the Galatian situation which warrants Paul's arguing the case for preexistence or incarnation, no heresy to combat. He does not suggest a doctrine of revelation (as is done in John 1:1–18) or derive a high priestly christology (as is done in Heb. 4:14–16) from his statement. Jesus' becoming subject to the law is important to indicate how those under the law are redeemed. Calvin says it simply: "By putting the chains on himself, he takes them off the other" (*Calvin's NT Commentaries: Galatians, Ephesians, Philippians and Colossians,* p. 74). The interchange, already mentioned (3:13–14), is effected, transferring prisoners from one control to another. Only this time, the resulting status for the prisoners is as God's children by adoption.

This passage (4:1–7, or at least 4:4–7) is often cited in lectionaries of Christian churches as a Scripture reading for Christmas Day or for the first Sunday following Christmas. It is interesting to reflect on the text in light of the holiday spirit when the sights and sounds of the season bespeak a joy often tinged with a romantic flair and yet when many are burdened with depression, emptiness, and disappointment. Try as they may, they simply cannot conjure up a feeling of celebration to fit the mood of angelic choirs and the wise men bringing gifts. The thought that they *ought* to be happy only compounds the despair. Verses 4–7 contain the note of joy, but only as Christmas leads to Good Friday and Easter, only as the baby "born of woman" redeems those under the law. God's humanizing presence in

> ... the stable where for once in our lives
> Everything became a You and nothing was an It
> (W. H. Auden, "For the Time Being")

includes also the cross and the tomb. The incarnation, as Paul depicts it here, entails a realistic solidarity with the depths of the human situation (even the situation of those depressed at Christmas) in order to change this situation. The good news lies not only in the announcement that a baby is born, but that "by putting the chains on himself, he takes them off the other."

(c) God also sends the Spirit of his Son to confirm the new

95

status of being his children. The coming of Christ effected the adoption, but humans, being what they are, need the certifying experience of Christ's Spirit so that they can actually address God as "Father." Just as an orphan taken into the home of foster parents may initially mistrust or at least wonder about the reception given by the new parents and may require some act or gesture to get over the feelings of being an outsider, so God's adopted children move about in fear until the Spirit operates at a deep level ("in our hearts") to corroborate not once but repeatedly the reality of the Father's love. Paul certainly means by "Spirit" something different from merely an esprit de corps or a general climate of toleration. One might come away from a successful meeting between two antagonistic groups and say, "A good spirit prevailed at the gathering," meaning participants were in a tolerant mood and refrained from bickering. But Paul has in mind specifically *God's* Spirit (or in this context, more precisely, Christ's Spirit), who functions in the lives of persons to bring them into the actual experience of being a member of his family.

Slaves become children, no more and no less. They are not stripped of their weaknesses and turned into spiritual giants so that they can chat with God on his level. Nor are they strangers at a gathering wandering about aimlessly because no one knows or cares about them. Paul stresses the ready access to the Father, the open door, the listening ear. It is somewhat striking to find here and elsewhere the phrase "Abba, Father" (cf. Mark 14:26; Rom. 8:15), which continues untranslated the Aramaic term "Abba" alongside its Greek equivalent. The early church obviously found something special in this intimate expression for God and preserved it in its original form. Jesus had used it in his time of great supplication (cf. Mark 14:36), and it may well lie behind the opening words of the Lord's Prayer (cf. Luke 11:2; Matt. 6:9). Not only did he as the unique Son face God with such intimacy, he intended his followers to do likewise. His Spirit makes it happen, overcoming the timidity of the newly adopted children and enabling them to pray in this unprecedented way.

The Holy Spirit is not to be thought of, then, as the obscure or even frightening member of the Godhead. He is, in the words of the Nicene Creed, "the Lord and Giver of life." He makes God real and alive to his people by unstopping their ears so they may hear and opening their mouths so they may pray.

96

What may otherwise degenerate into meaningless doctrine is animated so that one is drawn beyond a theory of adoption actually to say, "Abba, Father!" A whole new world of family relations, of freedom, of joyful obedience, of lively worship is opened up because "God sent forth the Spirit of his Son into our hearts."

(d) The way Paul writes in verses 4–6 raises the question as to whether he is also reflecting in some sense on the relationship of Father, Son, and Spirit, thus anticipating what later came to be the doctrine of the Trinity. God is the initiator who sends his Son and the *Spirit of his Son.* The activity of the Son is intended to make possible the adoption of others into God's family, but the Spirit is needed to complete this work by stirring the adopted children to call God "Father." The precise manner in which each of the three is connected to the other and particularly the way the RSV translates verse 6 (*"because* you are sons"; for another interpretation, see the NEB) suggests that the result is not coincidental.

Of course one must be on guard not to read into Paul the later theology of the church. The doctrine of the Trinity, which found expression in the councils of Nicaea (A.D. 325) and Constantinople (A.D. 381) and its influential exposition in the West by Augustine in the late fourth and early fifth centuries, is an effort to understand with the aid of Hellenistic philosophy the true diversity and undivided unity of Father, Son, and Spirit. God is three-fold in person but one in nature. Paul indicates no awareness of God's nature, his essence, his substance (4:4–6). He certainly does not speculate on an imminent relation of the three, how each member of the Godhead indwells the other. This way of putting the issue would have been as strange to Paul as it is to most modern readers. He does, however, assert a unified event of redemption in which Father, Son, and Spirit play diverse roles. In the single move to liberate an enslaved people God has acted through Jesus his Son and in the Spirit of Jesus.

The reality of the Trinity is both a mystery and mystifying. God always exceeds our comprehension of him; no creed or theology can encapsulate and explain him. The doctrine in its traditional expression, however, also tends to be unduly complex and mystifying. The decisive terms used in the ancient formulas are alien to anyone not trained in classical philosophy. For example, simply to say, "God in three persons" is a bit misleading since the Latin *persona* had a different meaning

97

from the English word "person." Recognizing the mystery of God, is there any functional way to "understand" the Trinity, to make sense of the biblical statements of Father, Son, and Spirit? Verse 6 of chapter 4 offers some help.

The phrase "Abba, Father" is a liturgical expression used in the Greek-speaking churches, preserving, as we have indicated, the intimacy of the address to God. In prayer God's children moved by the Spirit say, "Abba, Father." The context of worship, when the people of God respond in thanksgiving for their freedom, their adoption as sons and daughters, accomplished in Christ, provides the occasion for "understanding" the Trinity. The church in effect confesses its belief in the triune God when it prays—to the Father, stirred and strengthened by the Spirit (cf. Rom. 8:26-27), through the work and name of Jesus, the Son. It experiences the reality of God in action and acknowledges this by the way it says its prayers. Worshiping the one God in the awareness of his diversity does not relieve the church of the need of giving intelligible expression to the doctrine of the Trinity, but it does provide the proper starting point.

Galatians 4:12-20
An Appeal to the Heart

Throughout the letter to the Galatians, Paul makes various appeals to his readers to urge them not to succumb to the teachings of the agitators who have come into their congregations. At the outset he appeals to the authority of the one gospel which the Galatians had previously heard from him and had accepted. The gospel transformed Paul's own life and has been duly acknowledged by the Jerusalem apostles. He appeals also to the experience of the Galatians themselves, reminding them of their early days in the faith when the Spirit worked powerfully in their midst—not as the result of anything they did but as they faithfully responded to the message of the crucified Christ. Then Paul turns to the Old Testament to show how from the beginning God intended for Gentiles to be a part of Israel, but through Christ, not through the *torah.*

Yet another appeal is made (4:12-20), this time an appeal to the heart. The language is plaintive and tender. Paul recalls his first visit to the area and how eager and enthusiastic the

Galatians had been then in their response to the gospel and to him personally. They may have had reason to reject him, but instead they treated him royally as if he were a divine messenger. Has all of this gone? Is he now to be looked on with hostility? He can only agonize over them, as a mother suffers in giving birth to a child, in the hope that God will live afresh in them.

Because Paul writes from the heart to the heart, the paragraph does not flow like a logically constructed argument. One idea does not lead directly to another so as to build a climax. The thoughts and feelings are joined by the intense concern they express for the Galatians and their predicament. The outline below, however, indicates that while the appeal is emotional, it is not irrational.

(a) 4:12*a*.   Paul begs the Galatians to follow him in becoming free from the law.
(b) 4:12*b*–16. Paul reminds them of their initial reception of him and puts the ironic question as to whether he has now become their enemy.
(c) 4:17–18.   Paul accuses the opponents of having debased motives in courting the Galatians.
(d) 4:19–20.   Paul expresses his personal feelings of anxiety and perplexity and the desire to be present in Galatia.

The paragraph contains a high proportion of puzzling statements about which commentators are hesitant to make definitive interpretations. The reason for this can undoubtedly be traced to the fact that Paul is dealing with information which he and his readers already share and which needs only an allusion and not an extensive elaboration. For example, they both know the nature of Paul's bodily ailment, and consequently there is no cause for him to describe it in detail. Modern readers, naturally curious about Paul's physical condition, are unfortunately left in the dark.

Paul begins with an entreaty that the Galatians imitate him (4:12). Out of context the appeal sounds arrogant, as if he were setting himself up as a paragon of conduct to be copied by those in his churches. Why does he not suggest that they imitate Christ rather than himself? The point is not that he, Paul, is a model to be followed in all things. He rather argues that his acceptance of God's grace in Christ was in effect like becoming

99

a Gentile. He no longer stood under the suppression of the law. As with Peter, he came to "live like a Gentile and not like a Jew" (2:14). He urges the Gentiles in Galatia to follow him, to leave behind the enticement of circumcision (becoming like a Jew), and choose freedom as God's children. "Become as I am, for I also have become as you are."

Paul turns to reflect on the reception given him when he initially arrived in Galatia. Whatever the physical illness which originally led to his bringing them the gospel, it must have been the sort of sickness which could have caused the Galatians to reject him. The translation is uncertain, but the NEB seems to reflect the Greek text more faithfully than the RSV, ". . . and you resisted any temptation to show scorn or disgust at the state of my poor body" (4:14a). Though all identifications of Paul's infirmity are tenuous, one interesting suggestion is that he had an illness normally thought to be linked with demon possession. The Greek verb translated "despise" literally means "spit out," a gesture one used against the demonic influence on the sick. The Galatians, however, refused to be put off by such a threatening adversity (*if* that in fact was his problem) and received Paul not as demon-possessed but as an angel of God. Another suggestion explains the illness as a gross visual disorder, since Paul acknowledges that if it had been possible, the Galatians would have given him their eyes. This would entail taking 4:15 literally and not proverbially. It is not at all necessary to connect (though many commentators do) the illness mentioned here with the thorn in the flesh of II Cor. 12:7, also a difficult reference to identify. In any event, Paul and his readers can look back to his first contact with them with pleasure and gratitude.

"Have I then become your enemy by telling you the truth" (4:16)? It is an ironic question which hardly expects an answer. Paul knows why he is now viewed with suspicion, and the Galatians know, too. It is not because he preached the gospel to them faithfully and expounded its implications, but because of the itinerant missionaries who have arrived declaring a different message. Paul proceeds abruptly to charge them with unworthy motives in courting the Galatians' favor. They do not care about the Galatians, he argues; they only want to cut them off from all contacts so that the Galatians will end up envying and courting favor with them. Behind the enthusiastic regard the opponents are showing lies a selfish intention to satisfy their egos and make themselves the objects of the Galatians' attention. (See also the comments on 6:12–13.)

The imagery in the incomplete sentence of verse 19 is powerful but somewhat confusing (not unlike that in 4:1–7 or in Rom. 7:1–6). The Galatians are addressed as "my little children," but then in the birth analogy become embryoes still in the mother's womb yet to be delivered. Paul is the mother-to-be, waiting and suffering. In the latter half of the verse the expression "until Christ be formed in you" suggests a reversal of figures. Now the Galatians represent the pregnant mother and Christ the developing embryo. Despite the mixing of the roles, Paul succeeds in describing vividly the plight of the Galatians and his own feelings about them. They in accepting circumcision put themselves, as it were, back into the womb. They need a new birth. The experience of Christ's living in them must be cultivated afresh. As in verses 8–10, the acceptance of the false teaching is purely and simply a reversion to a pre-Christian state.

As for Paul, his feelings are a mixture of tenderness and anguish. These are his own children he is addressing. Once already, like a mother, he has suffered at their birth, and now he finds himself again in travail. How long will the labor continue? How long will it be before Christ lives again in them (cf. 2:20)? Perhaps being with them would help. Then he might find the right words, the right approach, to bring about the needed change. As it is, he feels helpless, at his wit's end to know what to say or what to do.

Verses 19–20 give a glimpse into the real struggles of Paul the pastor. Things have not gone right with his flock in Galatia. The attention they have been paid by, and in turn have paid to, the advocates of circumcision has led to their alienation from him and to the need for his risking a sharp, polemical letter like this in order to get them to see the folly of their ways. Though they have rejected his preaching and need now a completely new beginning as Christians, they are still his children. Anguish and tenderness are bound together with a puzzlement as to whether things will ever be different, whether the Galatians will rediscover the grace of God in its force and clarity, whether the relation between pastor and people will be restored. Few other places in his letters afford such a clear view into the heart of the pastor Paul.

Galatians 4:21—5:1
God's Promise and Christian Freedom

If in the previous section readers are given a glimpse into the distress and pain the apostle feels for his people, in this section (4:21—5:1) they are shown again the exegetical theologian interpreting the sacred text in a way that is immediately relevant to the situation. The two roles, however, should in no sense be severed—Paul as pastor and Paul as exegete. The very way he goes about introducing and applying this reflection on the story of Hagar and Sarah suggests that Paul has not thrown off the pastoral burden in taking on the mantle of the biblical scholar. Because the type of interpretation here seems forced to most modern readers, commentators tend to devote a great deal of attention to the method of exegesis Paul employs. How can he draw the conclusions he does from Gen. 21:9-11? But equally important as his handling of the Old Testament texts is his continuous probing and pushing to get the Galatians to see the radical character of God's grace. This section (4:21—5:1) at its simplest level might be thought of as two pictures Paul paints —one of Hagar and her offspring and the other of Sarah and her offspring—with the intention that the Galatians recognize themselves in the family of Sarah, that they find themselves mirrored in the children of promise. Then they can begin to act like the free people they really are and resist any pressures to be enslaved again. Paul as interpreter of the Old Testament stories is still Paul the pastor, confronting the texts not in a vacuum as a detached scholar but with the plight of his people very much in mind.

1. First, a look at the structure of the passage. It is basically composed of three parts: an introductory question, the allegory itself, and a concluding verse which serves as a bridge to the next section. The rhetorical question with which the passage begins reminds the readers in an explicit way of what has actually been demonstrated for them previously (3:6-14): The *torah* itself points to the promise of God's grace in Christ. It does not prescribe a state of servitude "under law" (4:21). If those who want to be faithful to the *torah* would only read it properly,

102

they would see that it acknowledges its own incompleteness and anticipates the fulfillment of freedom in Christ. In the second part of the paragraph (4:22–31), Paul reflects on the story of Abraham's two sons and their mothers and draws connections between them and the present situation. We shall examine how these connections are drawn later, but structurally it is important to note the two uses of the direct address ("brethren" in 4:28,31). They parallel each other and become the means by which Paul applies the allegory. Each is preceded by an Old Testament citation (Isa. 54:1; Gen. 21:10). The marginal reading of "you" in the RSV at verse 28 is greatly preferred over the "we" found in the body of the translation. The NEB, JV, TEV, NIV, and the three major editions of the Greek Testament choose "you" and relegate "we" to the margin. Finally, the first verse of chapter five, as the conclusion to the passage, is transitional. The first half of the verse provides a christological basis for the freedom of Isaac's children ("For freedom Christ has set us free"); the latter half issues a warning about returning to bondage ("and do not submit again to a yoke of slavery"), a theme continued in verses 2–12.

2. The allegory itself is drawn from Gen. 21:9–12. Abraham had two sons, but one was born of the maid-servant Hagar and the other of his lawful wife Sarah. The two mothers with their sons become contrasting types. Hagar is (somewhat mysteriously) linked with Mt. Sinai, and thus with the old covenant and with Jerusalem. This branch of the family, though it can trace its bloodline back to Abraham, remains in slavery and has no part in Abraham's inheritance. Sarah, on the other hand, corresponds to "the Jerusalem above," to freedom, to the inheritance. The key to the contrasting types comes in two pairs of phrases set against each other:

"according to the flesh—through promise" (4:23)
"according to the flesh—according to the Spirit" (4:29)

The birth of Ishmael happened in the natural process of events ("according to the flesh"; cf. NEB, "in the course of nature"; and JB, "in the ordinary way"). The birth of Isaac, however, was an extraordinary event because of Sarah's advanced age (so "through promise"). Isaac symbolizes the hope, Israel's future. This branch of the family is connected to the new age ("the Jerusalem above"), to birth "according to the Spirit," to freedom. Both lines go back to Abraham, but are clearly distin-

103

guished as to maternal source and to type of procreation. Paul declares that both he and his readers stand in the tradition of Abraham-Sarah-Isaac. Their life comes from the new age, where God who once fulfilled a promise to Abraham and Sarah about the continuance of their family has fulfilled another promise to Abraham—"In thee shall all the nations be blessed" (3:8; Gen. 12:3). It is through God's faithfulness, then, that Gentiles and Jews alike discover their freedom. Their identification as his people comes in their response to his promise, as Paul elsewhere states, "For not all who are descended from Israel belong to Israel, and not all are children of Abraham because they are his descendants; but 'Your descendants will be reckoned through Isaac.' This means that it is not the children of the flesh who are the children of God, but the children of promise who then are reckoned as descendants" (Rom. 9:6b–8).

One detail in the allegory needs additional comment. Verse 29 reads, "But as at that time he who was born according to the flesh persecuted him who was born according to the Spirit, so it is now." What persecutions does Paul have in mind? As far as the time of Ishmael and Isaac is concerned, the reference is probably to Gen. 21:9, where the Hebrew verb translated in the RSV as "playing" connotes mocking and jeering. Sarah demands that Hagar and Ishmael be expelled from the family because Ishmael has scorned Isaac. As for the persecution contemporaneous with the epistle, Paul is evidently thinking of the aggressive efforts of the opponents in Galatia who are pressuring his readers to be circumcised. As in the case of Paul's "persecution" of the Christians prior to his call (cf. 1:13,23), the verb may imply no more than an annoyance or a verbal harrassment. It would certainly be inaccurate to deduce from this verse any notion of a wholesale persecution laid on the Christians by the Jews. For one thing, Paul's polemic is not with the Jews but with Jewish Christians who argue the case for circumcision. For another thing, Jews showed little inclination to persecute Gentile Christians. They tended only to exercise synagogue discipline over those of their own number who converted to the Christian faith. The topic arises again later (5:16; 6:12).

3. What can be said for Paul's use of the Old Testament in verses 22–31? To readers schooled in historical interpretation, the passage is a puzzle since it makes connections and draws conclusions not hinted at by the writer of Genesis 21. If this were offered as a modern exegesis of the Old Testament passage, it would not be considered legitimate. Paul describes his

104

own interpretation as allegorical. By this he means that the story of the births of Ishmael and Isaac yields a meaning which lies beneath the historical account of the incident. In this respect Paul follows the exegetical methods learned in his days as a student of the *torah* where linkages such as those made in verses 22–31 would not have been at all unusual. The primary question, however, with any form of allegorical exegesis is whence comes the meaning underlying the historical account. For example, Philo, the Alexandrian Jew who is roughly a contemporary of Paul, also allegorizes the Hagar-Sarah story, but the meaning differs markedly from that of Paul. For Philo, Abraham represents the soul journeying toward a true knowledge of God. Hagar symbolizes the preparatory training of secular learning to which the soul must apply itself before the union with Sarah (i.e., divine wisdom) is fruitful. The underlying meaning of the story emerges from Philo's effort as an apologist to interpret the Jewish *torah* to a more philosophically minded Greek audience. Paul, on the other hand, thinks in terms of Israel's history and God's action in relation to this history, a history which for him is incomplete without the decisive chapter of Christ's liberating work. He is not concerned with general truths or moral principles but with parallels between God's dealings with Israel at the time of Abraham and his dealings with his people in the first Christian century. "The similarity between Isaac and the Christians was that the promise was the basis of their existence" (Ragnar Bring, *Commentary on Galatians,* p. 225). The underlying meaning, then, for Paul derives from his understanding of God's ways of working in the life of Israel, including his definitive work in Christ.

Another term needs to be set alongside the one Paul used. This section (4:22–31) is not only an allegorical interpretation of the Hagar-Sarah story, it is also a *midrash* on Gen. 21:9–12. Simply put, a *midrash* is an exposition of Scripture and came to designate for the Jewish people a body of commentaries on the *torah*. The intention of the exposition was either to clarify obscure elements in the text so that every word of Scripture could be more intelligible or to demonstrate the contemporary relevance of the text, how it applied in a new and changed context. Paul here does the latter. He provides a *midrash* on the Genesis text in the sense that his commentary has to do with the situation of the Gentiles in the Galatian context. He shows that the ancient story of Hagar and Sarah still has a function. It sheds light on the issue of circumcision facing Gentile converts. Isaac

105

and Ishmael were both circumcised (Gen. 17:25–26; 21:4), but what gives Isaac a place as Abraham's free heir is the fact that he was a child of the promise. "Now you, like Isaac, are children of promise" (4:28).

When he interprets the Old Testament, Paul uses methods for the most part strange to the twentieth century reader. In doing so, he follows in the tradition of rabbinic exegesis, and by comparison with others of his day (many more besides Philo could be cited) his methodology seems not at all eccentric. He is straightforward about describing his interpretation as allegorical, finding in God's relations with his people in the past a pattern (i.e., promise) which then sheds light on the current situation (4:22–31). The motivation for taking up the Genesis passage lies not in a speculative effort to decipher a riddle in the text but in the struggle to get the Galatian Christians to see themselves as free people, children of the promise, needing no rite like circumcision to help them relate to God.

4. Chapter 5, verse 1, though placed by some editors exclusively with verses 2–12 (so JB), has definite links with chapter 4 (4:21–31) and should at least be thought of as a transition linking the two sections together. The RSV provides a middle way by honoring the traditional chapter division and by making verse 1 into a separate paragraph. The connection with the allegory comes in the figure of Sarah, whose name is never used but who is referred to four times as "the free woman." Paul draws his reflections on the Old Testament story to a close by affirming who (i.e., Christ) has freed whom (i.e., us) and to what purpose (i.e., for freedom).

The language of slavery and freedom undoubtedly suggests itself to the New Testament writers as an apt description of God's work in Christ because of the history of the Jewish people. Israel became a nation by God's liberation of her from the bondage of Pharaoh and his leading her to a new land. When Jewish children asked their parents about the reason for the torah, they were to be told, "We were Pharaoh's slaves in Egypt; and the Lord brought us out . . ." (Deut. 6:20–25; 26:5–11). But it was a unique liberation unlike the numerous other occasions in ancient history when one nation escaped the domination of another. Israel became the direct property of God, a special people with a distinct identity. "For you are a people holy to the Lord your God; the Lord your God has chosen you to be a people for his own possession, out of all the peoples that are on the face of the earth" (Deut. 7:6). Israel was brought out of slavery for a purpose and a task (cf. Exod. 19:5–6). When Paul, then, uses terms like "slavery" and "freedom" to describe God's salvation in Jesus, he has in mind only secondarily the institution of slavery operative in the first century and manumission of slaves. More important is the pattern of God's action in Israel's history at the time of the exodus from Egypt.

"Christ has set us free" means that God's decisive salvation has been accomplished and a complete change of allegiances has been effected. No longer bound to task-masters like sin, the law, and death, Christians are set in the service of God. Like Israel, they become his possession, a special people whose identity comes in union with the liberator Jesus Christ. This is to say that more than their external situation is altered by the experience of being liberated. One could conclude from the manumission of slaves or the release of prisoners that nothing occurs but the removal of outside restraint. Yesterday persons were in chains and today they walk free. More than likely, however, they are the same persons, essentially unchanged. At the exodus and more crucially in Christ a deliverance happens which by its very nature is a transference from one dominion to another, with the remarkable result that the new bondage is perfect freedom.

Christian freedom, stated the way Paul states it, both overlaps with and sharply differs from many expressions of freedom found in common parlance and occasionally in theological discussion today. It is impossible to examine them thoroughly here, but a few of these varying expressions are worth noting in order to clarify Paul's thinking.

(a) For some, freedom primarily means the freedom to choose one of several options. At the ballot box people are free if they may vote for any candidate they wish. They are free if they may select a newspaper to read which has not been unduly restricted in printing the news. Certain restraints are always expected and in no way infringe on freedom if people themselves have a voice in determining what the restraints are. In like manner, people are said to be free if they may choose what religion, if any, they wish to follow, what sort of profession they want to engage in, what commitments to make. Such freedom is, of course, to be cherished. It is good that we choose our partners in marriage and do not have them chosen by our

107

parents. It is good that we have some choice in the form of government under which we live. It is bad to be manipulated, controlled, treated like puppets. God's sovereignty over us is not that kind of sovereignty. He, too, wants us to make free choices *for* him and *for* our neighbor. He gives us the freedom of choice. And yet to confuse this with Paul's statements about freedom is misleading. Augustine fought with Pelagius and Luther opposed Erasmus over just this issue. Whether examined theologically, sociologically, or psychologically, such a notion of freedom turns out to be very superficial, for human choices are never entirely free. Those who choose are always conditioned by a multitude of factors—heredity, culture, immediate environment, publicity, subconscious drives, and the like—and only deceive themselves if they think their choices are not determined in some measure. Madison Avenue learned that a long time ago. In contrast, Paul speaks of the bondage of sin and the restraint of the law (3:22–23). Freedom comes not in human choices but in a divine choice, in God's election of his people in Christ and their response in faith and obedience. The Gentiles in Galatia are not "free" to choose circumcision or not, as they will. The decision to be circumcised results rather in the loss of liberty, the return to bondage (cf. 4:8–11; 5:2–4). Paul's understanding of freedom is much more radical and realistic than merely the possibility of choice.

(b) Freedom can also be described as the absence of social, economic, or political oppression. A nation is freed when a tyrannical leader is overthrown and citizens can determine their own form of government. A class or group is liberated when economic exploitation, racism, or sexism is destroyed. Freedom consists in independence, self-determination, and at least the opportunity to make significant decisions without the duress of a coercive or patronizing authority. Christians have a high stake in freedom defined in this fashion. Their history has not always been a proud or distinguished one. Too often they have had to bear a share of the responsibility for a particular injustice or totalitarianism in that their action or acquiescence has contributed to intolerable situations like concentration camps, *apartheid,* and starvation. In addition, the Bible directs Christians to identify with the poor, the helpless, and the oppressed, and this in the modern world means taking part in movements that aim at human freedom and the alleviation of injustice. Such involvement is not optional. It is theologically

108

important in the struggle for liberation, however, to note a distinction between freedom as the removal of oppression and freedom as mentioned in 5:1. Success in correcting a social wrong does not mean bringing in the kingdom of God. Paul does not speak in Galatians of independence or autonomy. The coup d'état of the old age which Christ achieves, in fact, involves the establishment of a new regime of loyalty and dependency. Citizens are not free to determine their own destiny, but are claimed for service by the living, loving God, who immediately sets them in the fight against all dehumanizing tyrannies.

(c) Freedom can also be spoken of in a psychological sense, the removal of emotional barriers, the healing of past wounds, the coming to grips with internal forces so that one can control them rather than be controlled by them. The movement toward liberation entails the destruction of deterministic patterns of behavior in which the individual is caught so that creative instincts can emerge and decisions be more freely made. Again, Christians have a special interest in the efforts to enable persons to be fully functioning human beings. Jesus not only fed the hungry and preached good news, he also healed the sick and cast out demons. Furthermore, he commissioned his followers to do likewise. But is emotional health, as that is usually understood, to be equated with Christian freedom? A response to the gospel often produces in an individual various therapeutic effects, which are surely to be celebrated and cultivated. Unhealthy restraints and inhibitions which have thwarted personal growth and genuine relationships give way to a new openness and ease. Christian freedom, however, goes beyond this in linking individuals with the historical figure of Jesus. The aorist tense of the verb (5:1*a*) underscores this connection by pointing to a specific event in past time, literally "Christ liberated us" (cf. 3:13; 4:4–5). Freedom comes to Christians as a reality into which then they are called (cf. 5:13) and in which they participate. It is not an innate quality or state of being which the individual discovers (or recovers) by sorting out past experiences and relationships. It is a gift bestowed as a result of Good Friday and Easter, which accordingly involves the recipient in a concern for the total well-being of others.

(d) Freedom is occasionally defined as the quality of controlling one's own existence by a type of self-mastery. The Stoics, for example, taught that the individual could be liberated by curbing human passions and fears. In managing one's own soul a

109

person could develop a certain disinterestedness about the world and no longer be at the mercy of the ups and downs of life and history. Whether rich or poor, healthy or frail, an individual could achieve an inner freedom not dependent on outer circumstances. There are those today who would argue that a "free" person is one who never yields to one's feelings, who always meets tragedy with equanimity, and who is constantly in possession of oneself. Paul, in contrast, understands freedom not as retreat into the self but a liberation of the self from without. Christ who frees humanity refuses to withdraw from life, takes on the cross and sin of others, and suffers the consequences of his involvement. Christians take their cue from Christ so that self-mastery gives way to obedience and submission of the self to God. Therein lies the liberty.

Before leaving Paul's conception of freedom, two further observations need to be made. First, accepting the liberating work of Christ means rejecting any other offer that might promise ultimate freedom or security. This is why Paul urges his readers not to "submit again to a yoke of slavery" and warns them (5:2–4) about alternatives to the freedom of Christ. Not so much circumcision but larger defense budgets, expanded government programs, and the latest self-help books become today the basis for false hope. Jacques Ellul in a penetrating study of Christian liberty comments:

> The freedom which is given in Christ is radical insecurity from the human standpoint or from that of social structures and technical and political forces. For our only security is Christ. If, however, we seek and even accept some other protection or security, e.g., that of the state, or wealth, or social security, or socialism, or violence, or revolution, or justice, this will be a repudiation of our security in Christ and consequently it will be an alienation of our freedom. There can be no compromise here. . . . Freedom is both supreme insecurity and yet, as the whole of the OT reminds us, it is the only true security (*The Ethics of Freedom*, pp. 97–98).

The person who trusts the faithfulness of God is then in a position to take risks about everything else in life when the risks are valid expressions of Christian freedom (not obviously foolhardy risks which only indicate boredom or the need for attention). For Paul the risks come in the loving service of neighbors (5:13; 6:1–5)—including the risks involved in dealing with the economic and political systems which make some of them needy and hungry.

110

Secondly, because the life of faith is, at least from the human vantage point, an insecure life, Christian freedom should never be viewed as a privilege granted to a select few, a superior status for the elite. It is, in fact, an obligation entailing enormous responsibility. Slaves cannot be held accountable when they are crushed by powers beyond their control. They are not expected to behave like free persons when they are not. But once liberated, they are liable for the use of their freedom. They are answerable to a God who "is not mocked" (6:7). Like the people of Israel brought out of bondage through the Red Sea, there are moments of murmuring when the trials of freedom appear too demanding and by comparison the past in Egypt looks like a bed of roses (Exod. 16:3). The point is that the life of freedom can be uncomfortable, ambivalent, and even perilous. On the one hand, the burdens of others must be borne in love; on the other hand, free people must account for their own life and conduct (a paradox developed in 6:1–5). To experience the liberation of Christ is hardly the occasion for arrogant boasting.

Galatians 5:2–12
The Implications of Accepting Circumcision

"For freedom Christ has set us free; stand fast therefore, and do not submit again to a yoke of slavery." This first verse of chapter five, as we have seen, functions as a hinge connecting the argument of the allegory (4:21–31) to the urgent appeal Paul makes to his readers (5:2–12). It brings to a focus the theme of Christian freedom and how it is achieved by reminding readers that Christ is the liberator. At the same time, it issues an explicit warning about the temptation to lapse into bondage. The phrase "yoke of slavery" may reflect a common rabbinic expression "yoke of the *torah,*" used of proselytes as they assumed the responsibility of Judaism, but understood by Paul as a wearisome burden (cf. Jesus' play on this expression in Matt. 11:29–30). The section which follows sharpens the warning dramatically by setting forth the either-or character of the decision facing the Galatians and the grave consequences of choos-

111

ing circumcision. Nowhere in the entire epistle is the nature of the issue put so plainly and bluntly.

The case Paul makes is in the form of a personal entreaty (5:2–12), and for that reason the paragraph lacks a smoothly developed structure. Sentences tend to be short and in most cases rather abruptly linked to what precedes and what follows. Changes of thought are sudden and unexpected. The intense style fits the serious theme of the section, culminating as it does in Paul's caustic outburst in verse 12. Despite the almost staccato-like succession of phrases and expressions, however, the section is not totally without order and cohesion. The following outline calls attention to the various groups Paul has in mind and the way he moves from one to the other.

(a) 5:2–4.   The import of the decision facing *the Galatians who are at least contemplating circumcision.*

(b) 5:5–6.   The situation of *Christians ("we")* who in Christ await the completion of God's plan and thus find the circumcision-uncircumcision distinction irrelevant.

(c) 5:7–10*a*.   An expression of Christian confidence that *the Galatians* will finally resist the approach of the agitators.

(d) 5:10*b*–12.   An eagerness that *the agitators* ("he who is troubling you," "those who unsettle you") receive appropriate judgment.

First, a survey of the line of thought running through verses 2–12. The passage begins with a formal statement which gives to all that follows the flavor of an authoritative declaration. "Now I, Paul, say to you. . . ." "I testify again. . . ." Paul does not explain in what capacity he makes these personal pronouncements, for example, as apostle, as founder of the congregations in Galatia, or as Christian friend. The categories of course are not mutually exclusive. He certainly writes, however, as one who himself once believed in the cruciality of circumcision but has now discovered the way of grace (cf. 1:13–14; 5:11). His identification of himself ("we" of 5:5) with those in Christ who anticipate God's righteousness in the future and who no longer wonder about the importance of circumcision would suggest that he speaks from personal experience. He knows the inner logic and appeal of the argument that says persons are justified

112

in terms of the law; he was once an advocate of that position (5:11). Thus he has a certain right and authority to state how incompatible the position is with the gospel.

The declarations Paul makes about the Gentiles' reception of circumcision are unequivocal and to the point. "Christ will be of no advantage to you," "you are severed from Christ," "you have fallen away from grace." There is simply no way to tack circumcision on to the gospel of grace. It would mean that Christ died in vain (2:21). The opponents of Paul in Galatia evidently did not grasp the full import of their own teaching just at this point. They urged circumcision and certain calendar observances, but unlike zealous Jews did not themselves observe the law in its entirety (6:13). Paul, however, points out the inconsistency of such a position and states that one cannot isolate circumcision as a single necessary element of the law and dispense with the rest. He knows that circumcision symbolizes something very important—the identification of the Jewish people, the mark of those who live their lives under the jurisdiction of the *torah*. Thus when a Gentile receives circumcision, he declares his own identity in terms of the *torah;* "he is bound to keep the whole law." Thus for Paul the issue is serious and evokes uncompromising declarations.

The strong statement "you have fallen away from grace" (5:4)taken out of context often leads to misunderstanding. Paul speaks here of the dominion of divine favor into which God has summoned persons like the Galatians (1:6) and himself (1:15). If it is not in terms of their individual accomplishments or their innate attractiveness that God saves people but only because of his love, how can persons "fall from grace"? The answer is not that people forever lose God's mercy when they commit sins which for some reason they think are unpardonable, or when they grow lax in their prayer life and attendance at worship, or even when they act hypocritically. These are reasons often verbalized by individuals once active in the church who feel they have "fallen by the wayside." For Paul, however, it is only by seeking justification in the law that one "falls from grace" and finds himself cut off from Christ. God's gift by its very nature cannot be maintained by good behavior or religious activism or even wholesome sincerity. It can only be thankfully and joyfully received.   113

By shifting the pronoun to "we" (5:5–6), Paul contrasts the situation of Christians who comprehend the meaning of grace with the Galatian Gentiles who are contemplating circumcision. Stirred by the foretaste of God's new age in the presence of the Spirit, Christians await God's gift of righteousness. Rather than fully possessing it already, they live in hope and anticipation. Meanwhile, the question of circumcision is no longer a live issue for them. The position the agitators at Galatia have taken with their insistence on this visible symbol of security holds no appeal. It implies a demarcation between people based on a totally irrelevant and false distinction (cf. 6:15; I Cor. 7:19). What does matter is an active faith which expresses itself in deeds of love and care. We shall examine verses 5–6 in more detail later.

Paul returns to the Galatians (5:7–10a) and wonders that they could have begun their Christian pilgrimage so positively only to be led astray by trouble-makers. Who is it, he asks rhetorically, that thwarted your progress and kept you from faithful obedience to the truth? Obviously it is not God's work. A small amount of yeast affects an entire loaf (cf. I Cor. 5:6), and what has been advocated by these agitators has the potential of changing the whole face of the Christian community in Galatia. It is not to be taken lightly. Then with an abrupt shift from what has seemed like resignation about the plight of the Galatians, Paul expresses confidence that they will finally come around to seeing the issue the way he does. There may be a contrast intended between Paul's optimism (the emphatic "I" is used) which has its basis "in the Lord" and the persuasion of the opponents which "is not from him who called you." In any case, Paul has by no means given up on the Galatians.

In the final sentences of the paragraph Paul lets go his feelings about the false teachers who have disrupted the congregations in Galatia. These teachers are liable to the judgment of God because they have sought to divert believers from the path of faith (cf. Matt. 18:7; Luke 17:1–2). But what is more: "As for these agitators, they had better go the whole way and make eunuchs of themselves" (5:12, NEB)! This latter expression may be no more than an outburst of Paul's frustration over the activity of his opponents. On the other hand, castration is mentioned in the *torah* as a cause for excommunication (Deut. 23:1). Paul may be expressing his disgust in a way that has pointed meaning for the advocates of circumcision. Instead of ensuring inclusion in the people of God, let them carry their message further and be totally excluded!

114

Much of this section warrants more careful consideration than we have been able to give in the above survey. We shall select three verses for further comment.

1. In Chapter 5, verse 5 Paul exhibits a deliberate orientation toward the future. By the phrase "the hope of righteousness" he may mean the final acceptance of believers by God anticipated because of the present experience of righteousness in Christ, or he may have in mind the time of universal justice, mentioned so often in the Old Testament, when the cause of the poor and the oppressed will ultimately be vindicated. The one looks forward to the "not guilty" verdict God is to declare in the final judgment on those who by faith receive the gracious gift of a new relationship to him. The other depicts the era of peace when God brings vindication to those victimized by various tyrants and tyrannical systems. The two—the relational and the ethical—are not mutually exclusive and probably should be held together. In other letters Paul uses future tense verbs in connection with the revealing of God's righteousness or his justification of sinners (e.g., Rom. 5:17,19) and regularly depicts salvation as yet-to-be (e.g., Rom. 5:9–10). What is striking about verse 5, however, is that it represents the initial mention of the category of the future in *this* letter and in a way that appears sudden and unprepared for. Readers up to this point would assume that justification is an event which has already taken place or at least is taking place in the present. What is the effect of shifting to the future and of describing God's righteousness as something to be awaited?

(a) For one thing, a statement like verse 5 tends to tone down any frantic activism, whether religious or otherwise, which is either a misguided effort to win God's favor or an unbridled enthusiasm (as was the case at Corinth). Grace neither creates uncertainties about one's personal relation to God nor does it give cause for celebration at one's successes. As already indicated, verses 5 and 6 recount the situation of believers who have grasped the implications of God's grace and who no longer feel an enticement to the proposed safeguard of circumcision. They do not fret anxiously about their standing with God nor are they searching for a visible sign to make sure they have been included among the chosen people. They only "wait for the hope of righteousness." One might have expected Paul in such a context to say that the Spirit, normally associated with power, leads Christians to extraordinary deeds or acts of intense devotion. Instead, the Spirit prompts patience, a tarrying on God.

The notion of waiting connotes to most people of the West simply wasted time, minutes lost when the telephone lines are busy or longer periods spent impatiently because a friend is late for an appointment. One imagines all the things that one could be accomplishing. Paul's point is the reminder that the truly worthwhile accomplishments, however, are God's. His hoped-for righteousness cannot be forced by human achievements as if it were only the accumulation of so many kindly deeds. God will act to set things right in the world and to confirm the favorable judgment on his people, but it will happen in his own good time.

(b) Waiting for God's righteousness, however, does not mean passivity, indolence, and resignation. The word Paul uses carries the notion of eagerness, of lively expectation and is the same verb employed with great effectiveness in Rom. 8:18–25 (verses 19, 23, 25). There the process of waiting is compared to the labor-pains of the expectant mother, whose long time of pregnancy is coming to an end and who suffers not in despair but in hope. Those who have received the Spirit and who wait do so by sharing in the travail of a world looking for liberty and fulfillment. Here in Galatians Paul speaks of faith, striking the note of receptivity—but "faith working through love." Not under the delusion that their deeds win God's acceptance or coerce his plan for universal justice, Christians nevertheless prepare for the coming righteousness with deeds of various sorts (as mentioned in 5:13–14, 22–23, 25–26; 6:1–2, 6–10). The same Spirit who enables them to wait patiently also creates in them a restlessness with things as they are, a longing for the "not yet" of God's plan for the world. In the words of the beatitude, they "hunger and thirst for righteousness" (Matt. 5:6).

To speak of hope, then, is to speak of the thin line, as one has put it, between presumptuousness that cannot wait and despair that can only wait. It is a reliance on the promise of God that "he who began a good work will bring it to completion at the day of Jesus Christ" (Phil. 1:6), thus making the Christian life neither a precipitous effort to change the world nor unconcerned idleness. Paul will say more in the remainder of the chapter and in chapter six about the responsibility of freedom in Christ, but his discussion is incomplete without verse 5 and this striking reminder of God's future work. Faith and love find new depth when the third element of Paul's familiar triad, hope, is included.

2. In verse 6 of chapter 5 the expression "faith working through love" appears. In earlier sections of the commentary attention has been given to Paul's frequent use of the word "faith" and to the fact that it implies receptivity but not pure passivism. God has freely acted in Christ to save sinful humanity, an action totally unmerited and without parallel. The only appropriate response is acceptance, trust in God, complete reliance on his faithfulness. Yet if the response to such an amazing gift is genuine, faith cannot remain quiescent. The one who believes becomes aware of a community of believers and his faith is characterized by a concern for others, especially for those with a different history from their own. It is not against Paul but against a purely passive faith or a faith that had degenerated into credance that the Epistle of James was written, with its jarring words that "faith apart from works is dead" (James 2:26). For Paul as well, a decisive element of faith is obedience.

But the question arises: If faith must be active and issue in deeds of love, then has love become a precondition for grace? Does it function as a hidden but essential requirement for salvation? Has Paul, who has so vigorously opposed the idea of righteousness as a reward, brought in by the back door a justification granted only to those who show concern for their neighbors? By way of reply, two brief comments need to be made. First, the phrase "faith working through love" appears at the end of a long section in which Paul has taken great pains to argue that God's righteousness comes only as an act of his grace (3:1–5:12). That this righteousness which is received by faith clearly affects how the recipients live and act should be no surprise. That this righteousness is available only to those who have previously exhibited love would be implausible. Secondly, Victor P. Furnish has observed that the Greek participle in verse 6 may be taken as a middle voice ("working," RSV) or as a passive voice ("inspired," NEB margin); it may refer to love as the expression of faith or to God's love as the inspiration for faith. Furnish suggests that the two are complementary and further comments:

117

It has become evident that for Paul faith's obedience is an obedience in love, but an obedience which has the *character* of love because its ground is God's own love by which the sinner has been claimed and thus reconciled to God. The Christian is summoned to love in a double sense: to be *loved* and to be *loving.* Within the precincts of Pauline theology these two are inseparable (*Theology and Ethics in Paul,* p. 202).

"In Christ," where divine love is so profoundly experienced, believers find themselves to be vehicles bearing that same love to others.

3. Paul mentions "the stumbling-block of the cross" (5:11). The phrase is part of a somewhat isolated and enigmatic verse which presupposes a context shared by Paul and his initial audience but not clarified for later readers. Perhaps an opponent had accused Paul of being an advocate of circumcision or perhaps he was simply referring to his own past when as a Pharisee he had been an avid proponent of the *torah.* In any case, he asks rhetorically why if he were still urging circumcision would he be the object of harassment. To do that would make him acceptable to the opposition and no longer give them cause for being annoyed by him. At the same time, it would also mean that the preaching of the cross would lose its offensiveness and thus, for Paul, its power.

But why? What makes the cross a *skandalon,* a stumbling block? Paul's development of the theme in I Cor. 1:17–25 helps to explain verse 11. The idea of a crucified Messiah was a contradiction in terms for the Jew, since by definition the Messiah was to be a strong and successful leader who would bring deliverance to Israel. It was inconceivable that God's anointed could die such a shameful death (cf. 3:13; Deut. 21:23). For Paul, however, the very means of Christ's death symbolizes his power. Contrary to all rational explanations and external proofs, God makes this event of failure to be the occasion for saving his people. That Jesus was raised from the dead does not remove the element of scandal connected with the crucifixion; it only confirms it. Consequently, in his own preaching and teaching Paul is careful not to dilute the Christian message in order to make it more intelligible or palatable to his audience and so rob it of its redemptive power. "For Christ did not send me to baptize but to preach the gospel, and not with eloquent wisdom, lest the cross of Christ be emptied of its power" (I Cor. 1:17).

Theologically as well as personally the word of the cross is very important for Paul. It is a canon against which he measures

118

rival ideologies within the church. Thus in the Galatian context there is "an irreconcilable conflict between the cross, which was the revelation of salvation and was valid for all, even the Gentiles, and circumcision which was the sign of Jewish exclusiveness" (Ragnar Bring, *Commentary on Galatians*, p. 242). The two cannot be accommodated in a single way of thinking, and the Galatians are forced to choose.

Of course a pertinent question for modern readers is, Where in the nature of contemporary Christian experience does the theology of the cross expose similar choices? In what ways has the church in adapting to life in the twentieth century in effect removed the stumbling block of the crucified Christ? Have worldly criteria for success replaced the weakness and scandalous character of the cross? Where in seeking to make the gospel more palatable to an indifferent and skeptical age has its edge been blunted so that it bears little resemblance to the decisive message of the letter to the Galatians? To put the issue another way one may say, the Lord of the New Testament can be met *only* as the crucified Christ. He comes as the despised, rejected, weak, slain Messiah of Good Friday so that we either accept him as he is or altogether miss him. As such, of course, he contradicts the presuppositions people hold about what a deliverer should be and do. Helplessness, shame, and failure are no more a part of our religious expectations than they were of first century Judaism. What is more, responding to such a Lord implies not only coping with a historical figure of the past but with a continuing presence whose power is made known in weakness (I Cor. 12:7–10) and who still chooses the foolish to confound the wise (I Cor. 1:26–31). He remains an affront to systems, whether religious, social, or political, which seek in some way to fit him into their existing power structure or to adjust his teaching so that it suits the prevailing ideology. But to accommodate the gospel of the crucified Christ in this way is to remove the stumbling block—and the power—of the cross.

PART THREE

Freedom, Spirit, and the Life of Love

GALATIANS 5:13 — 6:18

The letter to the Galatians, though written with passion and at times expressing deep feelings, follows a remarkably logical design from beginning to end. Not only does it fit the standard letter form familiar from other Pauline writings (with the exception of the omission of the thanksgiving-prayer), but the argument in the body of the epistle unfolds in such a way that major divisions have a discernible and orderly relationship to each other. A section (like 5:1–12) may be comprised of disjointed sentences, but nevertheless it fits into an overall scheme in which the development of thought moves with clarity and force. In the greeting to his readers Paul states the theological basis on which his whole case rests (1:4) and immediately sets out to argue for the authority of the gospel, which he, the Galatians, and the Jerusalem leaders are obliged to heed. The narrative sections in the first two chapters, containing more autobiographical material than can be found in any other of his epistles, are not rambling reminiscences but serve to document the fundamental point Paul wants to make—the priority of the gospel. The end of the second chapter then introduces the important motifs of justification by faith and dying and rising with Christ, which in turn are elaborated in chapters three and four.

In the second major section (3:1—5:12) Paul goes back to the *torah* to document his argument that demanding circumcision for Gentile converts contradicts the essence of the Christian faith, and in doing so he discusses the status of the law now that the Messiah has come. The people of God find their identity not in the ceremonial rites mentioned in the *torah* but in union with Christ, where their familiar relations and their experience of true freedom are secured. Again, the end of this second major section touches on the issues to be developed in the following division of the letter—the warning about the maintenance of freedom (5:1), the mention of the Spirit (5:5), the description of faith as active in love (5:6), and even the reference to the stumbling block of the cross (5:11), which anticipates the conclusion (6:11–18). One might argue (and indeed many commentators propose) that the final section should begin at the first verse of chapter 5 and that verses 1–12 fittingly introduce what follows. Verse 1 has such a similarity to verse 13 in content as well as structure that the two must surely belong to the same major division. This way of dividing the letter is not without merit, but it fails to take account of the fact that the first verse (and in fact the entire paragraph 5:2–12) is oriented toward the issue of circumcision and its dire effects ("do not submit again to a yoke of slavery"), whereas verse 13 begins to suggest positively what the life of freedom involves ("through love be servants of one another"). A new phase in Paul's amplification of the gospel relative to the Galatian community is opened up with verse 13.

The section completing the body of the letter is characterized by exhortation. There are no less than fifteen imperatives or implied imperatives in the Greek text of this section (5:13—6:10), as Paul urges his readers to exercise their newfound freedom responsibly. Freedom is not a commodity obtained and stored away for a rainy day; it is a gift which increases its value in the using and can be lost through misuse. Specific and general advice, positive and negative commands are offered to give concrete substance to the manner of life which can be called both free and Christian. One must be careful on the basis of this feature of the section not to draw too precise a line between theology and ethics, doctrine and exhortation, as if Gal. 3:1—5:12 contains all the theology and Gal. 5:13—6:10 all the ethics. For Paul theology and ethics are bound up with each other in such a way that makes a sharp cleavage impossible. As we shall see, there is much good theology in 5:13—6:10.

The outline of the section is simple:

122

(a) 5:13–15.   Freedom means the loving service of neighbors.
(b) 5:16–26.   The Spirit is the mode and the power for the life of freedom.
(c) 6:1–10.   The responsibilities of the free and loving life of the Spirit.
(d) 6:11–18.   Paul's forceful postscript.

The last item in the outline (6:11–18) is not really a part of the body of the letter but a conclusion. Paul takes the pen from his amanuensis and in his own hand appends a note which epitomizes the letter as a whole and not merely the last major division. He is obliged to point the Galatians to the new creation, which transcends the Jew-Gentile distinction and where pride such as the agitators are exhibiting simply has no place.

The dominant theme of Gal. 5:13—6:10 comes in the command to love. Love is not another heavy load laid on believers like a new law to replace the one from which they have just been freed. Rather, love is the expression of true freedom. It comes as the fruit of the Spirit and has to do with bearing the burdens of neighbors. The interrelation of freedom, love, and the Spirit is addressed in a way that is particularly relevant to the situation of the Galatian readers.

The question is often raised as to what part Gal. 5:13—6:10 plays in the larger argument of the epistle. Does Paul add this later section in order to balance his more polemical presentation of freedom in the earlier chapters and thus guard against any misunderstanding which might arise? Contrariwise, is there a specific situation in the Galatian congregations which he here addresses by emphasizing love, the work of the Spirit, mutual help, and the constant need to do good? If there is a concrete problem addressed, how does it relate to the controversy over circumcision spoken to in the rest of the letter? These questions are not easily answered since Paul provides little information about the context of this concluding section. As we have seen in the "Introduction," one explanation postulates that he is fighting on two fronts against two opposing groups in Galatia. There are the advocates of circumcision, essentially legalists, and then there is a party of libertines, which holds to a view of freedom which disregards the commandment to love and every other restraint. The concluding portion of the epistle is directed to the libertines. While this particular explanation is sensitive to the topics Paul addresses in the letter, it finally raises more problems than it solves. There is no clear evidence that he changes audiences at verse 13 to deal with a second group of opponents. It is more judicious to argue that this section is intended for the same readership as the rest of the letter, but a readership which in living out its Christian calling in a pagan culture is faced with numerous external and internal pressures. In addition to the issue of circumcision, these Christians have to define their faith in relation to a society in which they exist as a small, relatively unknown sect whose theological and ethical direction is, for the most part, against the mainstream. The moral standards of the day diverge sharply from their own, and where outward conduct does resemble Christian practice, it is usually for very different reasons.

Thus Paul warns these Christians about abusing their God-given freedom and about destructive fighting among themselves. He strongly affirms the ethical relevance of the Spirit, as if this were a particularly needed emphasis. There is even a hint that he may be prodding them about their participation in the collection for the Jerusalem church (cf. 6:6,10 and 2:10). In the course of speaking to these concerns, Paul's presentation of Christian freedom takes on a more balanced character, but it is doubtful that he intended (in 5:13—6:10) merely to round out an otherwise one-sided argument. The paragraphs, while not so pointedly aimed at a single problem, nevertheless exhibit an immediate applicability indicating that the apostle still has the Christian communities in Galatia very much in mind.

This direct and specific dimension of 5:13—6:10 in a sense complicates the task of interpretation. On the one hand, the details of the Galatian situation are not clearly known to later generations. *Why* church members were fighting with each other (5:15) and *for what reason* they had failed to comprehend the ethical aspect of the Spirit's presence, interpreters can only surmise from hints here and there. On the other hand, Paul does not offer a set of moral principles, universally valid, which only need to be adjusted slightly and then applied to the modern context. The apostle never appears as an ethical idealist, but as a theologian who in writing to Christian communities interprets the meaning of the gospel for concrete issues. To move from Paul and the Galatian congregations to the present, or *vice versa,* can become a complex journey. Due to the social, cultural, and political gaps between the ancient and modern

124

worlds, it is rarely possible to find in the biblical text instant solutions to the moral dilemmas of the twentieth century. Terms like *inflation, capitalism,* and *over-population* do not appear in a biblical concordance. Our task in this commentary is first to overhear what Paul has to say to the Galatians, discerning as carefully as possible the circumstances he immediately confronts, and from Paul to be instructed about the meaning of Christian faith and life. It is often true that more ethical guidance can be gained from the biblical text by clarifying the underlying theological questions—the character of the God who is served or the nature and purpose of the Christian community—than by trying to locate passages in which there is a direct correlation between the past and the present.

Galatians 5:13–15
Freedom and Love

Jacques Ellul in *The Ethics of Freedom* writes:

> The glorious liberty of the children of God is not the happy fluttering of a butterfly from one attractive flower to another. It is joyous, but it is also radical, hard, and absolute. . . . Giving us our burden, God launches us into an unsuspected adventure, a conflict, which is finally that of freedom (pp. 124–25).

It is to this "radical, hard, and absolute" pilgrimage which Paul now turns in his letter to the Galatians. Already he has established freedom as a given, a divine deed effected when Christ exchanges places with humanity, taking the curse and granting the blessing (3:13–14). As in the deliverance from Egypt, God puts behind his people the bondage of the past; but then he begins to draw them into the future. What is a given becomes also "an unsuspected adventure," a movement beyond securities, comfort, and protection to the risks of love and the demands of service. Clearly there is a joy to the journey, but Ellul is right. It "is not the happy fluttering of a butterfly from one attractive flower to another." It is not an eternal high with its constant jubilation and triumph. For these initial readers freedom has to do with overcoming community strife, with nurturing gifts of patience, gentleness, and self-control, and with bearing one another's burdens. The refusal of circumcision is not the

125

only issue. There remains the vocation of living out the life of freedom.

The paragraph made up of verses 13–15 exhibits an unusual structure. "For you were called to freedom" (5:13a) provides a smooth beginning by concisely summarizing the message of the letter up to this point and in words recalling verse 1. The new section does not represent an abrupt break with what has preceded, even though it moves in a different direction. The word "only" signals the shift and introduces alternate ways in which freedom can be used: either as the occasion for self-indulgence or as a basis for a loving service of others. Verse 14 gives a reason for choosing the latter alternative. By loving, one fulfills the law, and Lev. 19:18 is cited to substantiate the point. While verse 14 readily follows 13, verse 15 seems tacked on. Without warning it changes the scene from a consideration of the relation of freedom, love, and law to the congregations in Galatia and offers a common-sense admonition about their continual bickering. "But if you bite and devour one another, take heed that you are not consumed by one another." The verse reminds modern readers that Paul is writing to an actual situation and is not disputing in a vacuum about irrelevant theological issues.

What is the occasion for this bickering in Galatia, which evidently had become rather vicious? With the words he uses, Paul paints a picture of a ferocious contest between wild animals, which can only end in mutual destruction. Because of the paucity of information, it is impossible to dogmatize on the cause of this in-fighting. At the same time, it is important to try to identify the historical situation as precisely as we can, since a knowledge of the context would enable us to understand more clearly what and why Paul has written as he has. Two solutions are worth consideration. One says that the squabbling has arisen out of the debate over circumcision. The proposal that Gentiles need, in effect, to become Jewish proselytes when they accept Christ has its opponents in the Galatian communities; and the two sides are at each other's throats. The only problem with this explanation is that Paul in confronting his readers over the circumcision issue never hints that there is a group in Galatia arguing his side of the case as well as a group siding with the agitators. He rather addressed them as a unity, only making an occasional comment to the agitators. The other solution links verses 15 and 26 and observes that the two verses immediately

126

precede and conclude the important paragraph emphasizing the ethical implications of life in the Spirit (5:16–26). The contention develops because some within the communities who have been possessed by the Spirit are led to pride and conceit (5:26) and perhaps even libertinism. They have been carried away in the exuberance of their experience and are in danger of turning their freedom into opportunities for the flesh by acting without restraint and by challenging their more timid colleagues. The communities likely began in a context of extraordinary spiritual activity (see on 3:1–5), but some members have failed to grasp what this means for moral decisions, particularly in a pagan society, and have instead provoked hostilities. This latter solution takes seriously the location within the letter of verses 15 and 26 and offers a plausible context for the interpretation of the entire section (5:13—6:10). The stress on love (5:13–14), *walking* by the Spirit (5:16, 25), the restoration of wayward brothers and sisters (6:1–5), and doing good (6:9–10) makes sense as appropriate notes to be sounded in the midst of such a controversy. The latter explanation for the bickering need not be chosen to the exclusion of the former. The people who are fighting are the same people who are confronted with the choice about circumcision, and it is unlikely that the circumcision issue is totally unrelated to the dissension. In talking about the Spirit's activity Paul makes two specific references to the law (5:18, 23).

We need a closer look at particular elements of verses 13 through 15 and their implications.

1. "For you were called to freedom." Not only does this clause facilitate a smooth transition, but by repeating the substance of the first part of verse one it clearly makes *Christian freedom the basis for ethics.* The aorist tense of the verb "call" reflects the same tense of the verb "free" in "Christ has set us free" (5:1*a*). The liberating work of Christ becomes the condition on which all else depends; without it Christian ethics cease to be Christian. This would be obvious from the context of the letter, but to remove any possible doubt Paul states it explicitly and without question.

What difference does it make? Why is the gift of freedom in Christ so important for human relations and practical moral obligations? One can live a decent life, refrain from destructive conduct, take up the cause of justice for others, even fight for the poor and the oppressed without Christian freedom. The

127

acts and behavior discussed by Paul and other New Testament writers can be performed on the basis of idealism, or in the belief that human nature is essentially good and needs only a slight push to improve itself. Extravagant deeds to better the conditions of the community, deeds that are astounding in the level of the sacrifice involved, can be done out of a sense of guilt or to achieve a particular political or social goal. When such actions do in fact make life more human and promote the cause of justice and peace, they are to be applauded and supported whatever the basis of the action (if one can even discern that). Certainly it is not the business of the church or any individual to measure morality and assess benevolent deeds to determine whether or not they are done in freedom. In fact, there is no sociological or psychological test to prove conclusively this aspect of human conduct.

What then is distinctive, even though it may not be perceivable, about the activity of the free community or free individual? Perhaps this is better answered by negatives.

(a) The deeds done in Christian freedom are not coerced or done to satisfy a legal demand. They are not pre-formed by a commandment or moral prescription so that the doers are obliged to keep their attention glued on what it is they are to do and away from the recipients of the deeds. Christ frees persons *from* such a law and *for* needy neighbors. To act in freedom is to be guided by the ones whose real needs are to be served.

(b) Free people are not determined in their actions by what sort of response their actions may or may not evoke. They are not miffed when a "thank you" is not immediately received for a contribution made or an important bill passed. They are not deterred when the recipients of a kindly deed do not all rush to vote democrat (or republican) or do not promptly become capitalists (or socialists)—or even reject Christianity. Christian freedom means the demonstration of freedom. Recipients may be witnessed to, but never compelled to answer in a particular way as if they are forever in debt to those who helped them.

(c) Free people are not deceived by over-valuing their moral decisions and their contributions to others as if their freedom depended on what they do. They know that freedom is a gift given, that to act freely is a sign of grace received, and consequently they do not have to be caught up in continually taking stock to see if enough money has been pledged or

128

enough service rendered. How much is "enough"? The characteristically Christian style of life emerges not so much in what is done as in the fact that what is done expresses the freedom given by God, whose call is to selfless, serving love. Such a vocation takes seriously the remarkable paradox expressed in Eph. 2:8–10 where the writer, after affirming that salvation comes by grace and not by works, adds: "For we are his workmanship, created in Christ Jesus for good works, which God prepared beforehand, that we should walk in them" (v. 10).

2. "Through love be servants of one another." Paul presents two possibilities for the use of Christian freedom. On the one hand, it can become "an opportunity for the flesh." The word translated as "opportunity" originally meant a starting point or a base of operations for an expedition. "Flesh," the source not only of immorality, licentiousness, and drunkenness but also of enmity, selfishness, and envy, is an opportunist who can easily make a beachhead on freedom's front with all sorts of dire consequences. Thus Paul bluntly commands the second alternative—mutual service in love. If freedom is the basis of Christian ethics, then *loving service is the proper exercise of freedom.*

What is immediately striking about Paul's way of putting it is the paradox between freedom and service (literally: "be slaves to one another"). Unfortunately, the paradox has lost some of its initial sharpness due to its familiarity in Christian usage, yet it can hardly be overemphasized. It recalls Jesus' conversation with the disciples when he said, "Whoever would be great among you must be your servant, and whoever would be first among you must be slave of all" (Mark 10:42–45). Likewise, Paul describes Christian freedom as a change of masters: "you who were once slaves of sin . . . have become slaves of righteousness" (Rom. 6:15–23). Such a statement cuts across the grains of any notion of freedom as autonomy and independence, yet it is indispensable for understanding God's action in liberating his people. As long ago as the deliverance from Egypt, Moses was directed to say to pharaoh in the name of God, "Let my people go, that they may serve me" (Exod. 9:1). It is not that God gives something (freedom) in order to take it back (be servants). Freedom has movement; it goes somewhere. It can lead to freedom for others or bondage. This orientation or direction of freedom Paul defines with the imperative.

129

The imperative ("be servants of one another") then has a

close relationship to the indicative ("you were called to freedom"). The two are not absolutely identified, but neither can they be neatly separated. The indicative always precedes the imperative, but also always leads to or implies the imperative. There is no way to talk about Christian freedom without at the same time talking about the command to serve. Victor Paul Furnish has commented:

> God's *claim* is regarded by the apostle as a constitutive part of God's *gift*. The Pauline concept of grace is *inclusive of* the Pauline concept of obedience. For this reason it is not quite right to say that, for Paul, the imperative is "based on" or "proceeds out of" the indicative. . . . The Pauline imperative is not just the result of the indicative but fully integral to it (*Theology and Ethics in Paul,* p. 225).

Think of the implications of what Paul commands. If I in love really become a servant to my neighbor, then I am delivered from the temptation of paternalism, of constantly being the wiser, richer partner who always knows what is best for my needy friend. I am at my neighbor's disposal and in serving him discover afresh the freedom God has given us both. He does something for me by providing me the occasion to look beyond my own problems, to be rid of my selfish preoccupations, and to find a liberating relationship. Must I then do everything he asks me to do, even if what he asks me to do seems destructive to him? No, because Paul qualifies his command: "*through love* be servants of one another." Elsewhere Paul describes love as that which "rejoices in the right" (I Cor. 13:6); it "does no wrong to a neighbor" (Rom. 13:10). I may on occasion have to oppose him, to challenge his ideas and commitments. He may in turn reject me, because he takes exception to the way our God liberates people so indiscriminately. Of course I must be careful not to give needless offense, not to take again the paternalistic mantle and be condescending, as if I were his master and he my servant. Love, however, must never shrink from conflict, lest it degenerate into mere sentimentality. Questioning his easy solutions and even jolting his intransigent principles may be the best favor I can do him.

3. "For the whole law is fulfilled in one word, 'You shall love your neighbor as yourself' " (5:14). There is something of a debate among the commentators as to the exact meaning of the verb "is fulfilled." Does Paul say here that the law is summarized in the one command "You shall love your neighbor as

130

yourself"? Or does he say that in love the law is obeyed and thus brought to completion? A parallel passage, Rom. 13:8–10, suggests that he may have both summarization and completion in mind. The citation from Lev. 19:18 clearly represents the essence of the law (though Paul regularly omits the command to love God mentioned in the Synoptic accounts, Mark 12:28–34; Matt. 22:34–40; Luke 10:25–37). He seems, however, to go beyond mere summarization by saying that the free life of love in reality (and of course in Christ) does fulfill the law. To put it in the words of the Romans parallel, "He who loves his neighbor has fulfilled the law" (Rom. 13:8). Thus *love puts the law in proper perspective.* It frees people from misuse through the law and frees the law from misuse by people.

Two comments about this. First, when Paul speaks of believers "loving," it is of a different order from saying they are joyful, or patient, or even just. Love is not one virtue among a list of virtues, but the sum and substance of what it means to be a Christian. In dying with Christ and in the subsequent new life, persons discover that they are recipients of God's love, and faith essentially means surrendering to this love (2:20; Rom. 5:5, 8). Only out of such surrender does the fulfillment of Lev. 19:18 become a reality. As we have seen (in connection with 5:6), being loved and loving are inseparable components within Pauline theology. Thus to say that the law is fulfilled in love is to take account of God's love in Christ. As sinners are placed "in Christ," they are remade by love so that they no longer are characterized by self-interest. "For the love of Christ controls us, because we are convinced that one has died for all; therefore all have died. And he died for all, that those who live might live no longer for themselves but for him who for their sake died and was raised" (II Cor. 5:14–15).

Secondly, love does not do away with the law but confirms it and provides its correct interpretation. Paul turns to the *torah* (Lev. 19:18) itself to find the "one word" which describes its fulfillment. The *torah* is not then destroyed but set in a new perspective by the command to love. Unfortunately, the interpretive role love plays is often misunderstood. It suggests to many nothing more than a way to get around the law, permissiveness, an excuse for doing whatever it is that one wants to do. The catch of course lies in the understanding of love, which for Paul is not to be confused with warm feelings or moments of tenderness. Love finds its true

131

expression in God's giving of himself in Christ (2:20; Rom. 5:6–8), and just such concrete and substantial self-giving lies at the heart of the command to love. The obligation demanded by the law is in no way lessened by love; it is instead made more radical and comprehensive. What is owed to neighbors is not the carrying out of a specific law but a total approach to life: continually being servants of one another. Love's claim is without restriction. The law, then, has value as a norm only in light of the dominion of grace, the power of love, and the new life of the Spirit.

Such an ethic controlled by love and based on the freedom of Christ will inevitably result in behavior which appears inconsistent, if not contradictory, particularly when compared with the rather predictable conduct dependent exclusively on the law. Decisions are made in terms of very specific contexts, causing a response sometimes to be Yes and other times No, even to the same request. I am not called to love "generally," but only particularly, and that means *this* man or *this* woman with his or her needs, pains, and interests. Paul's counsel on the issue of eating food offered to idols provides a good example. Having determined that there is nothing inherently wrong with the meat, his decision may be to eat or not to eat, depending on the conscience of the neighbor, "for whom Christ died" (I Cor. 8:11). Paul does not set out abstract principles which, if applied, may produce consistency, but directs his readers to an actual human being with unique circumstances. From each new individual and context Christians learn what precisely it is that love requires.

One final comment on the above discussion. Paul presumes a relationship between individuals. But suppose the one in need whom I am called to love is mired in a hopeless situation of oppression or poverty or exploitation. It is not Christian love if I ignore the social, economic, or political forces which have created the conditions under which this one lives and offer only palliatives or perhaps only spiritual support. In such an instance, love demands justice, and acts of love are transposed into efforts to bring relief from a form or forms of tyranny. Paul's immediate concern is with the personal relationship of the Galatian Christians, but the force of his command to serve one another in love carries broad implications for Christians' involvement in the cause of justice for all.

132

Galatians 5:16–26
Spirit and Flesh

Persons freed by Jesus Christ are given the vocation to love one another. Paul does not hesitate to state this calling in the form of a command, an all-encompassing command without loopholes, which claims the total attention of the ones commanded. There may be contexts in which it is difficult to determine exactly what love demands, but there are no occasions where the command can be set aside, no conditions under which Christians are obliged to do something less. But how is this command different from other commands of the law? Has Christ freed his people from the burden of one yoke to set them under another, heavier and more oppressive? Is love a new law? These questions about the Christian ethic have in part been answered in the way Paul relates freedom and love. Freedom is the basis for love, and love is the proper exercise of freedom. There is another point to the answer, however, which comes in verses 16 through 26. The Spirit dwells within Christians and, when allowed, produces the very love which has been commanded (5:22). It is not a mechanical action, mind you, but one in which the dynamic and direction are God's, so that in reality God makes possible the very life he demands. The results of the Spirit's presence fulfill Lev. 19:18.

Before looking to see how Paul discusses the Spirit's function in regard to Christian ethics (5:16–26), it is important to recall that this is not the only passage in the letter where the Spirit is mentioned. Paul has already reflected on the beginnings of the churches in Galatia when God supplied the Spirit and Christians received him in faith (3:1–5). We noted in the comments on the passage four features of Paul's presentation: (1) The Spirit comes in and with the preaching of the crucified Christ. (2) The Spirit is set in radical contrast to the flesh. (3) The Spirit is the power of the new age and thus the source of vitality and mighty works. (4) The Spirit comes to the whole community and not simply to a few, select leaders. The Spirit is identified with the blessing of Abraham which has come upon the Gentiles as a result of redemption in Christ (3:14). The new dominion, where

133

barriers are broken down and hostilities removed, where circumcision is no longer relevant, is marked by the promised Spirit. This is even more forcefully stated in chapter 4, verse 6, where God's sending of the Spirit is set alongside the sending of his Son to enable redeemed and adopted children to approach him with confidence. The Spirit functions so that ex-slaves can become aware that they stand in a changed relationship to God —now as children with their divine Parent in a new family. But this new existence is not expected to be easy. As with Isaac, children "born according to the Spirit" become the objects of harassment (4:29), but they are not left hopeless. The Spirit stimulates both the eagerness and the patience needed as they wait for God's righteousness (5:5). Meanwhile, the present is important because recipients of the Spirit have obligations to one another in community. They are to attempt the risky task of restoring brothers and sisters who have fallen away (6:1). Whoever follows the Spirit's lead in this and other affairs of the moment will then finally receive eternal life (6:8).

It is clear from this survey that Paul here (5:16–26) is not introducing his readers to the Spirit for the first time. Not only has the Spirit already figured prominently in the letter, but has been an integral feature in the Galatians' own experience. They are not like the early followers at Ephesus, who, according to Acts 19:1–7, had never before heard of the Spirit. As indicated (in the comments on 5:16), they likely engaged in sharp bickering precisely because they did not grasp the full implications of what life in the Spirit meant. Thus Paul's statements (5:16–26), while appropriate to his interpretation of the command to love one another, also serve as something of a corrective to the original readers.

The passage can be outlined as follows:

(a) 5:16–18. The opposition of the Spirit and the flesh.
(b) 5:19–21. The works of the flesh, which bar the way to the kingdom of God.
(c) 5:22–24. The fruit of the Spirit, which fulfills the law.
(d) 5:25–26. The command to walk by the Spirit—and some implications.

Let us first follow the flow of Paul's thought in this section. The RSV translation of verse 16 is a bit misleading. It treats the verbs in the verse as if they were both imperatives, parallel to one another ("Walk by the Spirit, and do not gratify the desires of the flesh"). The latter clause, however, is an emphatic future negative, conditional on the previous clause. Paul is saying, "Walk by the Spirit, and *then* you will never gratify the desires of the flesh" (cf. NEB and JB). The way to thwart the self-indulgence and sinfulness constantly at hand is to live by the Spirit. This then leads Paul to state how sharp the opposition is between the Spirit and the flesh (5:17). The "desires" of the one are bent on intercepting the "desires" of the other and of causing only frustration. Individuals may have perfectly good intentions to do something worthwhile, but when the flesh gets to work, it throws a monkey-wrench into the operation and prevents any action from taking place. This is reminiscent of the split Paul mentions between willing and doing in Rom. 7:15–20, where the law, though holy, just, and good, is unable to lead beyond sin. "But," Paul says, "if you are led by the Spirit, you are not under the law" (5:18). Here he returns to his characteristic use of the preposition "under," which has repeatedly been employed to express the plight of people prior to the coming of Christ or the plight of those Gentiles who may choose circumcision. They are "under the law" (3:23; 4:4, 5, 21) or "under a custodian" (3:25) or "under guardians and trustees" (4:2), which means being "under a curse" (3:10). The law for them acts like a dictator, demanding and condemning, but unable to grant freedom. The Spirit, however, not only provides the power to cope with the desires of the flesh, but also signals liberation from this legal tyranny.

The next two divisions of the passage carry the opposition of flesh and Spirit a step further by contrasting the results of each. "The works of the flesh are plain" (5:19). They cannot be hidden or mistaken. If inward in origin, they inevitably manifest themselves in action open to public view. Eight of the items included in the list are given in the plural suggesting visible conduct, for example, outbursts of hostility or strife, occasions of selfishness, drinking bouts. In case the obvious implications are not otherwise drawn, Paul issues the dire warning "that those who do such things shall not inherit the kingdom of God" (5:21). There is a fundamental incompatibility between life determined by the flesh and life in the reign of God.

In contrast, the Spirit leads to love, the very stance which the Mosaic law (5:14) and "the law of Christ" (6:2) demand; and with love come joy, peace, patience, kindness, goodness, faithfulness, gentleness or humility, and self-control. Interestingly, there is very little variation among the modern translators in rendering this list. The terms are straightforward and unam-

135

biguous. With some irony Paul adds that there is no law against such things. The Spirit, not the law leads to these results, which more than fulfill what the law itself requires. Furthermore, being "led by the Spirit" (5:18) is not a second, somehow deeper, commitment believers are called to make beyond their basic Christian vocation. "Those who belong to Christ Jesus" (one of Paul's expressions for Christians) have done exactly what he is urging in this paragraph; they "have crucified the flesh with its passions and desires" (5:24). They are no longer at the mercy of self-indulgence and sin.

The passage ends as it began, with the note of exhortation. Since the Spirit has brought life to the Galatians, has been accompanied in their midst by extraordinary deeds, has moved them beyond a slave mentality to the freedom of the Christian family, then they·must live by the Spirit. The Spirit must be allowed to be the mode and means of their life of freedom. The Greek word translated "walk" (5:25) differs from the one also translated "walk" in verse 16. In verse 25 a term with a military origin is used. "Follow the line of the Spirit" or "be in step with the Spirit's leadership" is something of the notion implied. Negatively, this means no self-conceit, no "challenging one another to rivalry" (NEB), and no jealousy. Positively, this means assuming responsibility for neighbors who by their own behavior are in an exposed position (6:1ff) and doing so in such a way as not to exhibit the self-conceit which seems a peculiar problem for those "who are spiritual."

We turn now to certain elements of the passage which need further clarification.

1. The word *sarx,* which the RSV renders as "flesh," presents difficulties to translators and interpreters. The NEB in this section consistently uses "lower nature"; the TEV prefers "human nature"; the NIV "sinful nature"; and the JB "self-indulgence." Each of these translations, with the exception of the RSV, chooses a different English expression for *sarx* when it appears in 3:3. What in fact are the meanings of the word? It often appears in the New Testament without any prejudicial connotation to designate a person's physical character ("flesh and blood," 1:16) or humanity as a whole ("all flesh," 2:16, literally) or the sphere of that which is human or natural ("in the flesh," 2:20) in distinction from what is divine or eternal. Since it is a part of God's creation, flesh is not thought of in these instances as evil or corrupt. It is not a far step, however, from

136

this last meaning to the meaning which carries a negative aspect: the individual or sphere which opposes God and consequently is sinful. Rudolf Bultmann draws a helpful distinction.

> Man, and hence the Christian, too, lives his natural life "in flesh." But the crucial question is whether "in flesh" only denotes the stage and the possibilities for a man's life or the determinative norm for it—whether a man's life "in flesh" is also life "according to the flesh"—or again, whether the sphere of the natural-earthly, which is also that of the transitory and perishable, is the world out of which a man thinks he derives his life and by means of which he thinks he maintains it. This self-delusion is not merely an error but sin, because it is a turning away from the Creator, the giver of life, and a turning toward the creation—and to do that is to trust in one's self as being able to procure life by the use of the earthly and through one's own strength and accomplishment (*Theology of the NT,* Vol. 1, p.239).

Sarx (5:16–24) is this historical, natural, earthly sphere from which people deceive themselves into thinking they can derive ultimate meaning. As such, it is the inveterate enemy of the Spirit, who comes as the power of God's new age and who leads ultimately to eternal life. To translate *sarx* as "lower nature" (NEB), "sinful nature" (NIV), or by the very ambiguous term "human nature" (TEV) is a bit misleading, as if Paul were implying that each individual is divided into two natures, a higher or spiritual side and a lower or fleshly side, which vie for control. There is indeed a conflict and the individual is one of the scenes where the struggle occurs. But Paul, thinking in the terms of the first century, has in mind two powers which oppose each other. The Spirit and the flesh in this context are not components of human nature but two realities on which individuals can base their existence, two directions toward which they can move. They can live "according to the flesh" or "according to the Spirit." To focus on one is death; to focus on the other is life and peace (cf. Rom. 8:5–6). In other contexts both are used as anthropological terms, but not in these verses (5:16–24).

What Paul means by the flesh needs a certain bit of translation for contemporary Christians. He is not saying that material things are inherently evil, nor is he implying that human feelings, physical desires, or sensual pleasures are themselves to be avoided or suppressed. What makes the flesh so destructive is that it can become the norm by which people's lives are lived. This world, with its measures of success and its rewards for hard work, absorbs all their interests and demands their full atten-

137

tion. There is no openness to God's activity, to the presence of the Spirit, to the life of the new age. The sum of things consists of what can be seen, handled, tasted—or bought. The flesh also has, as we have seen in connection with verses 1–5 in chapter 3, its religious expression. Circumcision, correct pedigree, or zealous piety can lead to "confidence in the flesh" (Phil. 3:3ff), and this may not be far from Paul's mind in verses 16–21. Of the fifteen items listed as "works of the flesh," eight have to do with conflicts of one sort or another, to which "spiritual" (without the capital "S") folks are not immune. Thus whether in its secular or religious expression, flesh defines that realm in which people think they can make their own mark in life and in so doing set themselves in opposition to God.

2. The coming of the Spirit involves a warfare, and humans become the battlefield on which the contest rages (5:17). The two powers "are opposed to each other." At the same time, humans are not merely the stage for the battle, they are also the ones being fought over. What is at stake is their own freedom, assured by the Spirit and yet challenged by the flesh. The particular part played by individuals themselves in this struggle is neither passive nor neutral. They have decisions to make which determine the course of the fighting. The quotation cited from Bultmann tends to stress the choices people make in seeking to find meaning in the world of the flesh. They allow themselves to be deluded into thinking the flesh, which is transient and perishing, can provide something more than corruption. Paul, therefore, does not hesitate to confront his readers with the command to walk by the Spirit.

We are again faced with the interrelationship of the indicative and the imperative (as in 5:13–15), God's gift and God's claim. But this passage sheds fresh light on the character of the command, which constantly confronts Christians in the course of their lives. To walk by the Spirit entails a genuine decision, but not a decision involving a strong effort of the will to overcome enormous obstacles in order to get something accomplished. Rather, Christians are called to entrust themselves to the Spirit, to God's activity, and simply to follow his guidance. It is not a reluctant Spirit who has to be persuaded or persistently begged to make available to us God's new world. The Spirit is, as it were, eager to function with power in the church and in individuals to produce his "fruit" and only needs to be allowed the opportunity. Paul's language, *"led by* the Spirit,"

138

"the *fruit* of the Spirit," "will from the Spirit *reap* eternal life," suggests not human abilities to accomplish extraordinary feats which then might be acceptable to God, but a simple openness to God's power to redeem and transform.

Before leaving the element of opposition existing between flesh and Spirit, it is necessary to recall that Paul has not established a dualistic view of the world in which two equal forces are locked in a struggle with the final outcome still in doubt. The struggle Paul depicts here (as well as in many other places in his letters) is in line with his view that the present evil age from which Christ has delivered his people still must be reckoned with. Its rulers, however, are doomed to pass away (I Cor. 2:6; 7:31) and cannot thwart God's purposes (Rom. 8:38). Sometimes the conflict grows fierce, but the ultimate conclusion is not uncertain (I Cor. 15:24). This is precisely the point Paul underscores: "For he who sows to his own flesh will from the flesh reap corruption; but he who sows to the Spirit will from the Spirit reap eternal life" (6:8). Furthermore, the flesh is not a power working in the same way as the Spirit. It never appears in the New Testament as the subject of an action unless somewhere in the context a statement about the Spirit also appears, while the Spirit regularly is affirmed as an acting subject with or without flesh being mentioned (cf. Eduard Schweizer, *Theological Dictionary of the NT,* Vol. VII, 132). In the modern world where so many conflicting claims are made on the lives of individuals and institutions, when one constantly contends with the reality of living "in the flesh" yet does not want to be controlled by the flesh, it is a salutary reminder that in the final analysis the flesh is no match for the Spirit.

3. Having looked at the flesh and the nature of the conflict between the flesh and the Spirit, we need to observe the results of the Spirit's actions. The first thing of note is that the word "fruit" (5:22) appears in the singular (in contrast to the plural "works" in 5:19), giving a cohesive and unified character to what the Spirit produces. It is not as if the Spirit in one individual creates love, in another joy, and in a third gentleness. To be sure, Paul speaks of the variety of the gifts in this way, the Spirit apportioning "to each one individually as he wills" (I Cor. 12:11). But the fruit of the Spirit is one and thus the list indivisible. At the same time, it is not coincidental that love heads the list. "It is 'love' which embraces and includes all the other 'virtues' which follow so that, no less than I Cor. 13:4ff. with which

139

it is strikingly parallel, this list may be regarded as a description of the concrete ways in which love is expressed" (V.P. Furnish, *Theology and Ethics in Paul,* p. 88). Love is not one characteristic of the Christian life which can be numbered alongside many others; it is inherent in what it means to be led by the Spirit and thus the quintessence of life "in Christ" (cf. 5:6, 13–14).

The list serves an important function. If there are those in the Galatian congregations who have been carried away by their ecstatic experiences of the Spirit and have become the occasion for controversy, this list calls them back to earth and to the fundamental activity of God in human lives. It contains, beyond the gift of love, a striking number of terms which have about them the mark of restraint and steadiness over against exuberance and self-assertion. For example, there is "patience," the quality of being long-suffering toward those whose conduct may in fact be calculated to provoke anger; there is "faithfulness," reliability in a world where one may often be the victim of another's unreliability; there is "gentleness" or "meekness," the avoidance of unnecessary anger or sudden brusqueness or self-assertion; and there is "self-control," the discipline of one's impulses and desires. The composite reminds those who tend toward an unbridled religious fervor or whose understanding of freedom partakes of a Dionysian spirit, that while love embraces joy, it must also cope with the ordinary and the ugly, with the arrogant and the ill-tempered. Life in community is never easy, and the promise here is that the Spirit will bring those specific qualities of love which make for well-being and peace.

The list also serves an important function in providing criteria for discerning the Spirit's presence. There are those in the church who avoid the concept of the Spirit entirely because it seems so subjective. They have heard a friend say, "I felt led by the Spirit to do this" and were horrified by what was being blamed on the Spirit. How can one be sure the cause was God's Spirit and not one's own neurosis or psychosis? How can the Holy Spirit be distinguished from our human spirit? A specific answer in every instance is impossible, but Paul provides help by saying that "the fruit of the Spirit is love" and by pointing to these descriptive marks of love. There may be no fool-proof method of documenting the Spirit's presence in human life, but we can follow his tracks by seeing evidences of love. If one's so-called "Spirit-led" activity ends in needless enmity, strife,

140

jealousy, and dissension, then it is a safe bet that the Spirit has had nothing to do with it.

Galatians 6:1–10
The Demands of the Spirit

At several places in the letter Paul writes a verse or series of verses which serve effectively as a transition from one section to another. Editors of printed translations often are baffled as to where exactly to begin and end paragraphs since the transition functions to conclude one passage and at the same time to introduce another. Verse one of chapter five is such a transition, as are verses 25–26. The latter brings to a climax the extended contrast between flesh and Spirit by exhorting readers to walk by the Spirit and to have no self-conceit, no provoking one another, no envy. But chapter six (at least 6:1–10) is so immediately connected to the transition verses (5:25–26) that it is difficult to know where to make the paragraph division. The Greek word for "Spirit," for example, which has been the major theme of verses 16–26, appears twice in verse 1 (in different forms) and twice again in verse 8. The injunction, "Let us have no self-conceit," could be the title for verses 1–10, with its stress on self-awareness and proper self-evaluation. The editors of the NEB obviously sense this latter connection (5:26) since they make verse 26 the beginning of a new paragraph (including 5:26—6:2). The RSV takes the cautious and perhaps wiser option in making verses 25–26 of chapter 5 a separate paragraph.

An outline for 6:1–10:

(a) 6:1–5.   Instruction in bearing the burdens of others.
(b) 6:6.   Injunction to support those who teach.
(c) 6:7–10. Encouragement to persevere in doing good.

Verse 1 presents a specific (though not necessarily actual) example of bearing burdens. A person, presumably a Christian, does something wrong. Those who walk by the Spirit are to restore him gently, all the while taking heed that they themselves not be tempted. The consideration of the example (which

141

is continued at 6:3) is broken by putting the action into a general imperative: "Bear one another's burdens, and so fulfill the law of Christ" (6:2). The verse recalls another place where Paul spoke of "the whole law" being fulfilled in the command to love one's neighbors (5:13–14). The intrusion of the imperative at this point interprets the act of restoration as an occasion of service by which the law of love is fully obeyed. Thus Paul is saying to a community which has experienced the life-giving presence of the Spirit and is contemplating circumcision in order to be faithful to the law, "Look! Take seriously your life in the Spirit. If you let the Spirit direct your behavior, you will be led to restore brothers and sisters in Christ who have fallen away. Then, as you share their burdens, you really will be fulfilling the law—the law of Christ."

Paul returns (6:3) to the specific example mentioned (6:1), at least to the attitude of those who are offering help. Attention to a wayward colleague can very easily breed a feeling of superiority, and so a warning is in order lest one think too highly of oneself. A self-evaluation which does not use the wayward colleague as a standard of measurement is more likely to prove realistic, not to mention the fact that the wayward colleague is then freed from being the object of comparison. The paragraph concludes with a reminder that each person "will have to bear his own load," likely a reference to the final judgment when each is to answer for his or her own life.

Verse 6 is something of a puzzle. First, what is meant by "all good things"? Is Paul encouraging a spiritual fellowship between teacher and pupil in which the two share together the depth of all they have learned in Christ? Or does "all good things" primarily refer to the financial support which pupils owe their instructor? A parallel passage in First Corinthians strongly supports the latter alternative. "The Lord commanded that those who proclaim the gospel should get their living by the gospel" (I Cor. 9:14). But, secondly, even if Paul has in mind financial support, what is the point of mentioning it here? What connection does it have with the section which precedes and follows it? Older commentaries often linked it with verses 7–10, making a single paragraph urging the support of teachers. This, however, is a difficult position to take in light of the flesh-Spirit contrast in verse 8 and the exhortation to do good to *all* in verse 10. One can only surmise that verse 6 is an isolated exhortation having to do with the catechetical situation in the Galatian congregations or that it possibly has some connection with the

142

collection Paul was gathering for the Jerusalem church. The collection is indirectly mentioned (2:10) and is not so farfetched as a reference here if read in light of Rom. 15:26–27. Speaking of the contributions of the Christians in Macedonia and Achaia to the poor in Jerusalem, Paul writes, "They were pleased to do it, and indeed they are in debt to them, for if the Gentiles have come to share in the spiritual blessings, they ought also to be of service to them in material blessings" (Rom. 15:27).

Paul encourages the Galatian Christians to persevere in doing good (6:7–10), but bases his encouragement on a foundation somewhat different from the foundation of other appeals and exhortations in the letter. It is not explicitly grace or love or forgiveness which here leads to good works, but the fact that God is not one to be trifled with. God is a just judge and operates on the notion that what people sows that they will reap. If they sow to their flesh, they will reap corruption; if they sow to the Spirit, they will reap eternal life. In light of the coming judgment when rewards will be made to those who have remained steadfast, readers are exhorted to do good. "And let us not grow weary in well-doing, for in due season we shall reap, if we do not lose heart" (6:9). There are no limits placed on the Galatians' efforts; they are to do good to all. In light of the trouble39-2ithin the community, however, special attention is needed for "those who are of the household of faith." With this admonition the main body of the letter comes to an end. Paul appends a forceful conclusion in his own handwriting, but the theme moves in another direction.

Now for a more detailed look at the two larger paragraphs of the section.

1. The instruction about restoring a fellow Christian who has done something wrong is remarkably perceptive. Whether Paul has in mind an actual case or not (the grammatical construction suggests a hypothetical situation), he certainly indicates an awareness of the problems of helping those in distress. The Greek word translated in the RSV as "overtaken" has about it the notion of "suddenness" or "surprise," and it is difficult to determine whether the individual involved has done wrong "on a sudden impulse" (NEB) or has been surprised in being detected (cf. RSV). In either case, he or she needs help. Whether or not that person is remorseful and repentant of his or her action seems not to be at issue. The "spiritual," presumably all Christians, are urged to engage in setting such an individual right. Paul may intend a certain pointed barb at those in the

143

Galatian congregations who make much of their spirituality ("you who are spiritual"), but if so, it is a veiled barb which does not finally exclude any in the church.

Church discipline is always liable to abuse, and Paul seems aware of this as he presents the example. First, the task is not that of punishment but of restoration. The main verb in verse 1 connotes a remedial action: to return one to an original state, to reconstruct something which has broken down. There is no hint of retribution or punitive action. Christians are not urged to set up a tribunal to see that the guilty party pays for his or her sins. (In fact Christ has already done that!) Secondly, the restoration is to take place "in a spirit of gentleness." This phrase may mean no more than a mood of gentleness, or as several modern translations read, "very gently." But it has been noted that the phrase is in fact a Semitic way of saying "the gentle Spirit" (cf. Rudolf Bultmann, *Theology of the NT,* vol. I, p. 337). Thus Paul may have in mind the energizing work of God's Spirit, one of whose marks is gentleness (5:22–23). The tenderness and care needed in restoration come from the one most offended, God, who does not leave Christians on their own in the task but promises to be present intimately in the healing process.

Thirdly, and in more detail, Paul warns Christians to be aware of themselves as they engage in helping another. In the very middle of a verse (6:1) addressed to "brethren," he switches from the plural "you" ("you who are spiritual") to the singular ("Look to yourself, lest you too be tempted") to make the point even sharper. Each individual is warned to be wary, not about the neighbor and his needs, but about oneself. Realistic self-evaluation, Paul suggests, is a guard against falling into temptation and puts one in a position to help with the burdens of another. Self-satisfaction and complacency produce a patronizing arrogance, where one is only too ready to call attention to the faults of others but blind to his own. "Thank God, I am not like this publican!" To avoid self-delusion, each is to "test his own work" and to refrain from focusing on the problems of the neighbor. Paul evidently feels confident that any accurate self-assessment will indicate that one's own work is plagued with sin and can hardly provide sufficient cause for boasting. There will simply be no grounds for self-conceit (5:26). Whether thinking of future difficulties on earth or contemplating the final judgment, the reminder that each "will have to bear his own load" (6:5) tends to promote humility.

144

It is in the paradox of bearing one another's burdens and bearing one's own load that church discipline and Christian service must operate. The very idea of restoring one "caught in any kind of wrong-doing" (TEV) sounds a bit strange to modern ears. The current mood is more one of live-and-let-live, of staying out of other people's business, of avoiding friends who seem constantly to want to take care of us. There have been too many in the past who have been only too eager to put us right when we have gone astray. But Paul describes the restoration as bearing burdens: sharing the pain of failure, assuming a portion of the guilt and judgment, particularly in the process of making amends. Christians become so involved in the situation of the neighbor that they must take care not to be tempted themselves. But this mutuality only happens when those who help are aware of themselves, their own needs and weaknesses, and have not forgotten their own accountability. This description of church discipline is a far cry from the inquisitions of yesteryear or the sharp condemnations of moral magistrates or even the disapproving glares of the self-righteous. The image "body of Christ" connotes this profound mutuality where members have "the same care for one another. If one member suffers, all suffer together; if one member is honored, all rejoice together" (I Cor. 12:25–26). It is an example of what it means to walk by the Spirit. Luther expresses this beautifully:

> If there is anything in us, it is not our own; it is a gift of God. But if it is a gift of God, then it is entirely a debt one owes to love, that is, to the law of Christ. And if it is a debt owed to love, then I must serve others with it, not myself. Thus my learning is not my own; it belongs to the unlearned and is the debt I owe them. My chastity is not my own; it belongs to those who commit sins of the flesh, and I am obligated to serve them through it by offering it to God for them, by sustaining and excusing them, and thus with my respectability, veiling their shame before God and man. . . . Thus my wisdom belongs to the foolish, my power to the oppressed. Thus my wealth belongs to the poor, my righteousness to the sinners. . . . It is with all these qualities that we must stand before God and intervene on behalf of those who do not have them, as though clothed with someone else's garment. . . . But even before men we must, with the same love, render them service against their detractors and those who are violent toward them; for this is what Christ did for us (*Luther's Works,* "Lectures on Galatians —1519," vol. 27, p. 393).

145

2. In the second long paragraph (6:7–10) of this section, Paul, somewhat surprisingly, sets before his readers the coming judgment, when decisions are to be made based on the lives and

actions of people, not exempting Christians. At other places in the letter, the judgment has been alluded to (5:2, 21; 6:5), but only here is it elaborated and specifically made the basis for exhorting the Galatians to continue in their well-doing. Paul uses the imagery of reaping, which in the Bible becomes a technical term to signify the harvest of the final judgment (cf. e.g., Job 4:8; Joel 4:12–13; Rev. 14:14–16; Matt. 13:30; Mark 4:29). Four times in this paragraph the verb appears and always in the future tense.

Furthermore, verses 9–10 are more pointedly oriented toward the final judgment than is evident in English translation. One of the Greek words for "time" *(kairos)* appears twice, rendered by the RSV as "due season" (6:9) and as "opportunity" (6:10). In the former case, the "time" is that of the judgment when God confirms the believer's faithfulness in walking by the Spirit and obeying the command to love. Likewise, the word carries the same orientation to the future (6:10). "Thus, as we have opportunity in (6:10) does not mean: *Whenever*, from time to time, it may be possible to do good, we should do it. It means, rather *as long as* this present eschatological time continues, it is in fact the time to love, and we should be obedient in love" (V.P. Furnish, *The Love Command in the NT*, p. 101).

But what are we to make of this judgment by works? How is it to be squared with Paul's emphasis on God's grace and justification by faith?

(a) The first thing to note is that the mention of judgment does not represent an isolated slip of Paul's pen (6:7–10), as if he as a Christian knows better but occasionally lapses into the ways of an orthodox Pharisee. At various places in his letters he calls attention to the day when "we must all appear before the judgment seat of Christ, so that each one may receive good or evil, according to what he has done in the body" (II Cor. 5:10; cf. I Cor. 3:12–13; 4:5; I Thess. 4:6; Rom. 2:6–10, 16; 14:10; etc.). Clearly this includes Christians as well as non-believers. The notion appears so often that it cannot be dismissed as an idea from Paul's Jewish past which somehow he cannot let go. The final judgment plays an important, though not frequently mentioned, part in his Christian thinking.

146 (b) Secondly, Paul does not use the fact of divine judgment to strike terror into the hearts of his readers and threaten them into believing or behaving. He consistently looks on the judgment of believers with a certain amount of confidence. "God

has not destined us for wrath, but to obtain salvation through our Lord Jesus Christ," he writes in a context where he has previously declared that "the day of the Lord will come like a thief in the night" (I Thess. 5:2, 9). The reason for confidence lies in the judge of that final day, who is no less than Jesus himself (cf. Rom. 5:9; 8:31–34; I Cor. 1:7–8). As W.G. Kümmel has noted, "Paul saw the expectation of the judgment in the context of the message of salvation" (*The Theology of the NT,* p. 230). He can say unqualifiedly to the Roman Christians, "There is therefore now no condemnation for those who are in Christ Jesus" (Rom. 8:1).

(c) Christians in the face of the judgment are to strive to verify the gracious work of God in them. They are under no delusion that their efforts will save them; in fact, Paul seems to distinguish between the plural "works" as a futile attempt to win God's favor and the singular "work" as God's action in Christians (cf. 6:4; Phil. 1:6; I Cor. 3:13). Faith active in love is freed from the former but deeply involved in the latter and in so doing attests its own genuineness. What Christians will be asked about in the coming judgment is the integrity of their life in Christ, how their faith has expressed itself. Paul put it in the form of an exhortation to the Philippians: "Work out your own salvation with fear and trembling; for God is at work in you. . . ." (Phil. 2:12–13; cf. Eph. 2:8–10).

This sobering word written to the Galatians (6:7–10) reminds them that they cannot presume upon God's grace, as from time to time Israel of old had done. They cannot grow lax and take God for granted. They cannot let faith degenerate into mere credence or the cultivation of warm feelings. In the time remaining until the judgment, they must keep on being obedient in love and being faithful in their service of all, within the church and without, and so verify their calling. In the final analysis there is no basic contradiction in the fact that God is both gracious and righteous, both loving and just. He who in mercy justifies the ungodly is the same God who inquires about the obedience of faith.

Galatians 6:11–18
A Concluding Postscript

It is not surprising that Paul who has dictated this letter should take up the pen and add a postscript in his own handwriting; it was his custom (cf. I Cor. 16:21; II Thess. 3:17; Col. 4:18). What seems unusual is the nature and tone of the appendix. No other epistle contains such a lengthy concluding remark (unless Rom. 16 is to be taken in this category) and all without intimacy or personal greetings. Instead, Paul chooses to return to the primary reason for writing and to several terms already mentioned in the body of the letter: circumcision, flesh, law, the cross of Christ, boasting, and persecution. The section, in fact, epitomizes the heart of the letter. Paul wants to make no mistake about the issue pending before the congregations of Galatia and puts his full weight behind a firm decision on their part (6:17).

An outline of the conclusion:

(a) 6:11.   Paul's acknowledgement of his own writing.
(b) 6:12–13. Accusations about the motives of the opponents.
(c) 6:14–15. Boasting in the cross of Christ and the affirmation of the new creation.
(d) 6:16.   The first blessing.
(e) 6:17.   Paul's final appeal.
(f) 6:18.   The second blessing.

The opening verse of the section calls attention to the importance of what Paul wants to say. The "large letters" in which he writes are probably not due to poor penmanship caused either by eye difficulties or some other ailment. It is more likely that he uses larger script (as one today might use capital letters or italics) to be sure that his readers do not miss his closing words. "Take good note of what I am adding in my own handwriting and in large letters" (JB). Though an outline may not indicate it, the paragraph which follows exhibits a remarkable cohesiveness in that not only conjunctions but repeated words link one sentence to another. For instance, verses 12–13 are about the agitators in Galatia and their motives, which Paul then contrasts with himself. By repeating the verb "glory" (6:13 and in 6:14) and by using a conjunction ("but"), he provides a clear connection between the two longer units of the paragraph. Likewise, the first blessing (6:16) is smoothly joined to the preceding verses by a conjunction (not expressed in the RSV) and with the phrase "by this rule." Only verse 17 presents any sort of break in the flow of the paragraph, but even then the underlying reason for Paul's appeal ("for I bear on my body the marks of Jesus") relates to the earlier theme of persecution for the cross of Christ. Verses 11–18 are no hasty or ill-conceived postscript.

Paul makes two accusations against the opponents in Galatia (6:12–13). First, they advocate circumcision, he says, in order "to make a good showing." They are far more interested in what can accrue to their own account by virtue of successful proselytizing than what happens to their proselytes. They even "boast of your having submitted to that outward rite" (6:13, NEB). Secondly, by compelling the circumcision of Gentile converts, they avoid persecution "for the cross of Christ." Being able to report progress in their work lessens the pressure and removes the harassment they would otherwise be experiencing. One can only guess that the pressure on those Jewish Christian opponents comes from militant, nationalistic Jews who resent the biracial character of the Christian community and thus promote a missionary zeal for circumcision. If the Jewish Christians can show that they are making Jewish proselytes from among the Gentile converts to Christianity, then they need no longer fear their more ardent and exclusivistic compatriots. Exactly how intense the pressure and how fierce the persecution it is difficult to determine. The Greek verb for "persecute" here may imply no more than "annoy." What was probably at stake was the standing these Jewish Christians sought to maintain within the Jewish community and the fear that in becoming Christians they would be ostracized from their own people (cf. D.R.A. Hare, *The Theme of Jewish Persecution in the Gospel According to St. Matthew*, pp. 60–61).

In contrast to their boasting of their success in proselytizing and their aversion to persecution, Paul sets his own cause for boasting, the cross of Christ, and later, his own marks of suffering (6:17). This identification with Jesus' death means that the world, its mores and standards, its enticements and rewards, has been put aside. It no longer acts authoritatively for Paul nor determines his status. In its place has come a brand new world,

149

where neither circumcision nor lack of it matters. Those who will live according to the new creation, who will walk according to this "canon," receive God's blessing of peace and mercy.

At the close of the blessing (6:16), Paul adds "and upon the Israel of God," the only occurrence of this expression in the New Testament. There is a difference of opinion among commentators as to whether he intends by this phrase to include (a) all the Jewish people (cf. Rom. 11:25–26); (b) the faithful within Judaism whom God will ultimately save; or (c) the church now joined with the people of the old covenant to be "the Israel of God." Grammatically the issue is complicated by the word order in the Greek and the appearance three times in the verse of the connective *kai* ("and," "also," "even"). In light of Paul's efforts to redefine God's people as those who belong to Christ (3:6–29), the third option (c) seems the most plausible. This is reflected in the RSV (and JB, NIV), where "all who walk by this rule" and "the Israel of God" are understood as two descriptions of the same group, not two groups. Paul is affirming that "the Israel of God" now includes those who have been crucified with Christ and live in his new creation, even uncircumcised Gentiles. (For a different interpretation, see the NEB.)

Having examined the structure of the postscript and followed the flow of Paul's message, we need now to face three crucial questions of interpretation, which lead us to the heart of the passage.

1. What does Paul mean when he says that the world has been crucified to him and he to the world? Since he uses the first person singular pronoun, many interpreters have read verse 14 (like 2:20) as relating a private mystical experience, peculiar to the apostle, which at best other Christians can only hope to approximate. He relates, so it is said, a personal happening like the vision of paradise and the thorn in the flesh, mentioned in II Cor. 12:1–7. The interpretation of verse 14 as a mystical experience, however, fails to take note of the context. Paul writes in the first person singular so as to draw a contrast between the opponents in Galatia and himself. They take pride in the success of their proselytizing efforts; he takes pride in the cross of Christ. It is thus natural for him to speak of "me" and "I," but the pronouns need not be understood in an exclusivistic sense. Furthermore, Christ's death, which is the occasion and means of Paul's death to the world, and *vice versa,* is no private, inner experience, but a historical event, dated somewhere around A.D. 29–30. At the same time, it is also an inclusive event

150

in which God's people by faith participate. Paul simply affirms that part of the meaning of the death of Christ is that by it the world has been crucified to him and he to the world. It is the truth about all who are united to Christ.

By "world" here Paul means not the universe created by God but "the present evil age" (1:4), the enslaving dominion where "the weak and beggarly elemental spirits" rule (4:9), the sphere in which barriers between Jew and Greek, slave and free, male and female still exist. It is from this control that freedom has been granted. Robert C. Tannehill comments:

> The world has a structure which determines the life of each individual, and so human life as a whole, and man can only escape from this through an event which breaks into the all-encompassing world of sin and opens the possibility of a new existence in a new world. It is to such an eschatological event that Paul is referring when he speaks of the crucifixion of the world (*Dying and Rising with Christ*, p. 64).

But Paul significantly uses the perfect tense of the Greek verb "crucify," indicating that this world about which he speaks is not entirely over and gone. He still has to contend with it and live his life in a "crucified" relationship to it (cf. 2:19–20). He meets it when he shops in the marketplace and travels the roads of Asia Minor and Greece. He sees its effects in the faces of beggars and in the conniving of the prosperous. Its pleasures and pains are never far away.

Inevitably the world's presence creates two critical tensions with which those who like Paul live this "crucified" relationship must cope. First, there is the tension of living in the world with its carefully worked out authorities, standards, and schemes and yet as those who answer an alien authority, recognize contrary standards, and follow a plan which leads against the stream. Living lives of freedom from the world and daring to serve neighbors in need can only bring Christians into conflict and affliction. For Paul there were "the marks of Jesus" which he bore in his body (6:17), evidently the scars and injuries resulting from his missionary preaching (cf. I Cor. 4:11–13; II Cor. 4:4–5; 6:4–6; 11:23–26). His life, however, sounds a bit dramatic for most Christians, who hardly picture themselves as heroes in such unusual circumstances. And yet there is, even for "ordinary" Christians, no way to avoid the acute pressures. They may come as sharp confrontations with the world, or as a slight but steady tension, or as opposition which only flares up from time to time. Of course as long as they remain merely

151

religious, Christians can stay on good terms with the world. The world tolerates and even values much of what is represented by religion, its rites and its forms. The opponents of Paul in Galatia found that fostering a ritual like circumcision would enable them to avoid persecution. But being crucified to the world is not synonymous with being religious. It connotes subjection to a different authority, "our Lord Jesus Christ," by whose cross this new relation to the world has come about.

Perhaps it is important to add that this conflict with the world is not something Christians seek as if it will prove their faithfulness. It is not to be confused with masochism, or its more heroic form, "the lust for martyrdom." Those who hunt for fights in order to be able to suffer for Christ's sake only expose their own sickness, not their dedication. Neither is it to be misconstrued as a principle of mortification, whereby one looks around for something to sacrifice for the faith as if asceticism were the essence of Christianity. The conflicts with the world will indeed come. One need not search for them like Easter eggs hidden behind rocks and among bushes. The only question is whether Christians, like the Galatian agitators, having met opposition, then flee and take refuge in compromise or even capitulation, or whether they face it honestly.

A second tension created by the continued presence of the world is an inner tension. It may emerge during a skirmish with the world or in anticipation of it or more often in the aftermath of it. It comes because Christians, though participants in Christ's death, at the same time are still subject to temptation. Though crucified to the world, they are not immune to doubts and fears, to the anguish of uncertainty, to questioning their own commitments. The Gentiles at Galatia were experiencing just such an inner struggle as they were offered the promise of security in circumcision. As Paul put it to them, a great deal was at stake (cf. 5:2–4). If there are not the intellectual doubts about this or that item of the faith, then there are the practical doubts because God seems distant or prayer useless or despair overwhelming. In the final analysis, can God be trusted? Is grace really sufficient for all human needs? Could the world's standards and systems be right after all? Living in a "crucified" relation to the world in no way prevents or even lessens these haunting, human questions. In fact, being engaged in conflict may tend to intensify them. But Christian existence does not finally end in uncertainty or despair. Paul even in this context describes it with a note of joy. "Far be for me to glory except in the cross of our Lord Jesus Christ" (6:14)—which leads to the second crucial question of interpretation in this passage.

2. What does Paul mean by "glorying" in the cross of Christ? The Greek verb is one of the apostle's favorites and is generally translated "boasting." In many contexts it carries a very negative connotation. Boasting is the essence of self-reliance; independence from God; pride in one's heritage or specialness or performance under the law. It is foolhardy to "rely upon the law and boast of your relation to God" (Rom. 2:17; cf. 2:23; 4:2). All boasting has been excluded by the character of grace in God's dealings with people. The response to a divine relationship is not pride, but faith (Rom. 3:27). Consequently, the opponents in Galatia show their true colors when they make a boast of their success in compelling Gentile converts to be circumcised (6:13). In contrast, however, to this form of self-righteousness and arrogance, there is an appropriate and positive sense in which Christians can boast. They can "boast of the Lord" (I Cor. 1:31; Rom. 5:11) or, as in 6:14, they can boast in the cross of Christ.

Briefly three comments need to be made about such positive boasting. First, Paul can talk confidently of the cross because he sees it in the light of Easter. This one with whom he is united in death he knows as the victor over death, the servant who is "our Lord Jesus Christ." In the letter to the Galatians, very little is said about the resurrection; it is explicitly mentioned only in the first verse. But it is assumed throughout. To be crucified with Christ means that even now in this world of the flesh where tensions are acute "Christ lives in me" (2:20). Thus the cross is not an occasion for grief, but for boasting. Secondly, in terms of human experience this boasting carries with it a remarkable attitude toward hardships and afflictions, those pressures which come from conflict with the world. In the face of a more aggressive group of antagonists at Corinth who were accusing him of cowardice, Paul writes, "I will all the more gladly boast of my weaknesses, that the power of Christ may rest upon me" (II Cor. 12:9). Without denying the perplexities during his times of affliction and even acknowledging on one occasion that he was so unbearably crushed that he despaired of life itself, Paul finds meaning in suffering. It becomes an occasion for experiencing the transcendent power of God "who raises the dead" (II Cor. 1:8–10; cf. 4:7–12; Rom. 5:3). The

153

external pressures resulting from a hostile world and the inner tensions of doubt and uncertainty give way to a single-minded boasting in the cross of Christ. Finally, Paul's understanding of the cross not only creates a positive attitude toward his own trials and tribulations but also enables him to identify with suffering humanity. In a passage like II Cor. 1:3–7 he can draw a direct connection between Christ's afflictions and comfort, his own afflictions and comfort found in Christ, and solidarity with the afflictions of others, which makes possible comfort also foı them. The sufferings of Christ provide the basis for a community where troubles and pains are shared and where divine consolation is mediated.

3. What does Paul mean by "a new creation"? From the context of 6:11–18 and from parallel passages in other epistles, we can gather several clues which help to illumine its meaning.

(a) First and foremost, the phrase recalls a promise which in various forms the prophets reiterated to Israel. God was to do a new thing for his people. Sometimes it is pictured as a new exodus from bondage (cf. Isa. 42:9; 43:18–19), at other times as a new heaven and a new earth (cf. Isa. 65:17; 66:22). As an event, God's action was to be decisive, ultimate, and final so that "the former things" which had thus far sustained Israel could be forgotten. It would involve not merely a renewal or a restoration but an altogether new creation. This, Paul says, is precisely what has happened in Christ. Instead of a world where sin roams freely and law is a custodian, there comes a dominion where Christ rules as Lord, where the Spirit functions to keep life human, where freedom replaces bondage. To participate in the death and resurrection of Christ is to be brought into this new creation, where one can "walk by this rule" (6:16). Christian existence means living in the midst of the old world (as we have seen in connection with 6:14) but as a member of this radically new order, as God's *avant-garde.*

Understood in this light, the translation "creation" (RSV, NEB, NIV) is preferred to "creature" (TEV, JB). Paul clearly intends a contrast with "the world" *(kosmos),* mentioned twice in verse 14. It is not simply that an individual has been drastically changed so that he or she can be described as a new man or a new woman. Paul is thinking in broader terms than the inner transformation of this particular person or that. Rather with the death and resurrection of Christ a whole new world has been created, which exists simultaneously to and in conten-

154

tion with the passing world. Individuals do at some point in their histories become aware of their citizenship in this new creation and drastically change as they enter it and live in it, but it is not limited to or dependent upon their transformation.

(b) A second clue to the understanding of the new creation is to be found in the close relationship between verses 15 and 14. The conjunction "for" indicates that Paul (6:15) is giving a reason for glorying in the cross of Christ, through which the "crucified" status toward the world has come about. This means that the new creation cannot be understood apart from Christ. Certainly the other appearance of the phrase in II Cor. 5:17 confirms this observation. "When anyone is united to Christ, there is a new world" (NEB). Furthermore, in the Ephesian and Colossian letters another expression is used for God's new order —*kainē anthrōpos,* best translated as "a new humanity"— which is even more thoroughly linked to Christ. He creates "in himself one new humanity" (Eph. 2:15), and in baptism converts "put off" the old humanity and "put on" the new (Eph. 4:22–23; Col. 3:9–10) as in Galatians they "put on Christ" (3:27).

The point is that the new creation must be understood christologically. In the Galatian context that means directing one's life not by the law but by the crucified and risen Lord. Christians are rare birds in that an existence interpreted this way will at times appear just as foolish and just as much of a stumbling block as the cross itself. To some of the world's citizens they will seem too passive and patient, to others too meddlesome and aggressive. When the prevailing mood is uncritical optimism, they will likely be pessimistic; when discouragement and gloom abound, they may sound optimistic. They perceive, for example, that the Christ with whom they are united has a special affection for the poor and the oppressed, and consequently they are obliged to meet him among the poor and the oppressed (cf. Matt. 25:31–46; Isa. 58:1–9). This will undoubtedly seem a strange place to choose to be. Christians simply take their cues from one who was "for others," whose life and death lead them repeatedly to use the phrase "for us."

(c) The negations which begin verse 15 give us a third clue. "For neither is circumcision anything, nor uncircumcision" (6:15). The terms refer not merely to the rite administered to male Jewish babies and to proselytes or the lack of the rite, but to the categories of people distinguished by it. Earlier in the letter Paul has spoken of himself as a missionary to the uncir-

155

cumcised and Peter as a missionary to the circumcised. His point is that these distinctions no longer count in the new order. In place of hostility and division, in place of Jew and non-Jew, there is unity. He essentially repeats the word put so effectively earlier: "There is neither Jew nor Greek . . . for you are all one in Christ Jesus" (3:28).

The implications are clear. The new creation is a corporate reality, a community whose members are characterized by their accepting attitudes and actions toward each other. II Cor. 5:16–17, written to a congregation whose partisanship was a serious problem, spells out this feature even more pointedly. "With us therefore worldly standards have ceased to count in our estimate of any man; even if once they counted in our understanding of Christ, they do so no longer. When anyone is united to Christ, there is a new world; the old order has gone, and a new order has already begun" (NEB). Living in the new creation involves finding a way of regarding people differently than in the old order, where race, nationality, sex, economics, and the like provide categories by which individuals and groups are valued. It means no longer "using" people as an occasion for selfish boasting. Instead, they become recipients of a service offered in love, neighbors to be cared for, those for whom God's mercy is freely given.

"The grace of our Lord Jesus Christ be with your spirit." The closing benediction follows a pattern familiar from other Pauline letters (I Cor. 16:23; Phil. 4:23; I Thess. 5:28; II Thess. 3:18; Phile. 25; cf. Eph. 6:24; Col. 4:18). It is an often used blessing. In the Galatian letter, however, it has special significance. What Paul asks for them in this prayer is no less than what he has urged them to accept throughout the preceding six chapters, grace as the foundation for life. As he began (1:3, 6), so he concludes.

SELECTED BIBLIOGRAPHY

1. Recommendations for further study of Galatians:

BARTH, MARKUS. "Jews and Gentiles: The Social Character of Justification in Paul," *Journal of Ecumenical Studies* 5:241–67 (1968). Focusing on Gal. 2:15–21, Barth advocates an understanding of justification as a social event and discusses the implications for the church.

BEKER, J. CHRISTIAAN. *Paul the Apostle* (Philadelphia: Fortress Press, 1980). A recent study of Pauline theology, stressing the triumph of God as the central theme of Paul's gospel.

BETZ, HANS DIETER. *Galatians: A Commentary on Paul's Letter to the Churches in Galatia,* HERMENEIA (Philadelphia: Fortress Press, 1979). A thorough examination of the text as an example of the "apologetic letter"; likely to become an influential work on Galatians.

BRING, RAGNAR. *Commentary on Galatians,* trans. Eric Wahlstrom (Philadelphia: Muhlenberg Press, 1961). An extremely perceptive commentary, stressing the theological issues dealt with in the epistle; unfortunately it is currently out of print.

BULTMANN, RUDOLF. *Theology of the New Testament,* trans. Kendrick Grobel, 2 vols. (New York: Charles Scribner's Sons, 1954, 1955). The section in volume one on Pauline theology is a classic.

FURNISH, VICTOR PAUL. *Theology and Ethics in Paul* (Nashville: Abingdon Press, 1968). An important study, stressing the theological, eschatological, and christological character of the Pauline ethic.

HUNTER, A. M. *The Gospel According to St. Paul* (Philadelphia: Westminster Press, 1966). A popular sketch of Pauline theology; particularly helpful for lay people needing an introduction to Paul.

KÄSEMANN, ERNST. *Perspectives on Paul,* trans. Margaret Kohl (Philadelphia: Fortress Press, 1971). Contains several of Käsemann's essays; profound, occasionally difficult to read, but always creative and provocative.

KECK, LEANDER E. *Paul and His Letters,* PROCLAMATION COMMENTARIES (Philadelphia: Fortress Press, 1979). A lively study of the major aspects of Paul's theology; excellent scholarship; succinctly written.

LUTHER, MARTIN. "Lectures on Galatians 1519," *Luther's Works,* Jaroslav Pelikan, ed., Vol. 27, 151–410 (St. Louis: Concordia Publishing House, 1964) and "Lectures on Galatians 1535," *Luther's Works,* Vols. 26 and 27, 1–149. Clearly the most important and most influential study of Galatians.

STENDAHL, KRISTER. *Paul Among Jews and Gentiles* (Philadelphia: Fortress Press, 1976). A challenge to the traditional understanding of Paul; stimulating and eminently readable.

TANNEHILL, ROBERT C. *Dying and Rising with Christ* (Berlin: Verlag Alfred Topelmann, 1967). A thorough examination of a central theme in Pauline thought; exegetical in nature.

2. Other works cited in the commentary:

AUDEN, W.H. "For the Time Being," *The Collected Poetry of W. H. Auden* (New York: Random House, 1945).

BARTH, KARL. *Church Dogmatics* (Edinburgh: T. & T. Clark) Vol. IV, Part 1 (1956) and Vol. IV, Part 3, Second Half (1962).

BARTH, MARKUS. "The Kerygma of Galatians," *Interpretation* 21:121–46 (1967).

CALVIN, JOHN. *The Epistles of Paul the Apostle to the Galatians, Ephesians, Philippians and Colossians,* David W. and Thomas F. Torrance, eds. (Grand Rapids: William B. Eerdmans, 1965).

CULLMANN, OSCAR. *Peter: Disciple, Apostle, Martyr* (Philadelphia: Westminster Press, 1962).

ELLUL, JACQUES. *The Ethics of Freedom,* trans. & ed. Geoffrey W. Bromiley (Grand Rapids: William B. Eerdmans, 1976).

FORSYTH, PETER TAYLOR. *The Principle of Authority* (London: Independent Press, 1952).

FURNISH, VICTOR PAUL. *The Love Command in the New Testament* (Nashville: Abingdon Press, 1972).

HAY, DAVID. "Paul's Indifference to Authority," *Journal of Biblical Literature* 88:36–44 (1969).

HARE, DOUGLAS R. A. *The Theme of Jewish Persecution of Christians in the Gospel according to St. Matthew,* SOCIETY FOR NEW TESTAMENT STUDIES MONOGRAPH SERIES 6 (Cambridge: Cambridge University Press, 1967).

HOWARD, GEORGE. *Paul: Crisis in Galatia,* SOCIETY FOR NEW TESTAMENT STUDIES MONOGRAPH SERIES 35 (Cambridge: Cambridge University Press, 1978).

JEWETT, PAUL K. *Man as Male and Female* (Grand Rapids: William B. Eerdmanns, 1975).

KÄSEMANN, ERNST. *Jesus Means Freedom,* trans. Frank Clarke (Philadelphia: Fortress Press, 1972).

———. *New Testament Questions of Today,* trans. W. J. Montague (Philadelphia: Fortress Press, 1969).

KÜMMEL, W. G. *The Theology of the New Testament,* trans. John E. Steely (Nashville: Abingdon Press, 1973).

MOLTMANN, JÜRGEN. *The Church in the Power of the Spirit* (London: SCM Press, 1977).

SANDERS, JAMES A. "Torah and Paul," *God's Christ and His People,* Jacob Jervell and Wayne A. Meeks, eds. (Oslo: Universitetsforlaget, 1977).

———. "Torah and Christ," *Interpretation* 29:372–90 (1975).

SCHÜTZ, JOHN H. *Paul and the Anatomy of Apostolic Authority,* SOCIETY FOR NEW TESTAMENT STUDIES MONOGRAPH SERIES 26 (Cambridge: Cambridge University Press, 1975).

SCHWEIZER, EDUARD. *"sarx,"* *Theological Dictionary of the New Testament,* Gerhard Kittel and Gerhard Friedrich, eds. (Grand Rapids: William B. Eerdmans, 1971), Vol. VII, 98–151.

WILCKENS, ULRICH. *"upokrinomai,* etc." *Theological Dictionary of the New Testament,* Gerhard Kittel and Gerhard Friedrich, eds. (Grand Rapids: William B. Eerdmans, 1972), Vol. VIII, 559–71.

ZIESLER, J. A. *The Meaning of Righteousness in Paul,* SOCIETY FOR NEW TESTAMENT STUDIES MONOGRAPH SERIES 20 (Cambridge: Cambridge University Press, 1972).